MARGARET FEINBERG

GOD'S
POWER
IN ME

★ ★ ★ ★

52 DECLARATIONS AND
DEVOTIONS FOR KIDS

ZONDER**kidz**

ZONDERKIDZ

God's Power in Me
Copyright © 2021 by Margaret Feinberg, LLC

Requests for information should be addressed to:
Zonderkidz, *3900 Sparks Dr. SE, Grand Rapids, Michigan 49546*

ISBN 978-0-310-74461-0 (hardcover)

ISBN 978-0-310-74712-3 (ebook)

Library of Congress Cataloging-in-Publication Data

Names: Feinberg, Margaret, 1976- author.
Title: God's power in me: 52 declarations and devotions for kids / Margaret Feinberg.
Description: Grand Rapids: Zonderkidz, 2021. | Audience: Ages 8–12 | Audience: Grades 4–6
   | Summary: "God's Power in Me is an interactive 52-day devotional that encourages young
   readers 8–12 to break free from negative thinking and focus on the positive truths of who
   God made them to be. Through daily devotions paired with a 90-second affirmation kids
   can say aloud every day, readers will grow closer to God and learn to challenge the personal
   doubts that might be holding them back. I'm not good enough. I don't deserve to be their
   friend. And things will never change. Kids tell themselves things like this every day, and
   popular Bible teacher and speaker Margaret Feinberg wants to help them defeat those self-
   doubts and stop believing the lies because God only tells us the truth about ourselves, and
   that truth is we are all meant to have a joyous and powerful life. Throughout the devotions in
   God's Power in Me, kids will discover quick daily affirmations they can hold on to, biblical
   teachings, and practical applications for their own lives, Inspiration to banish any negative
   thoughts and ideas they may have, and encouragement to stand in their own truths while also
   growing closer to God in the process"—Provided by publisher.
Identifiers: LCCN 2021009131 (print) | LCCN 2021009132 (ebook) | ISBN 9780310744610
   (hardcover) | ISBN 9780310747123 (ebook)
Subjects: LCSH: Christian children—Religious life—Juvenile literature. | Self-talk—Religious
   aspects—Christianity—Juvenile literature. | Affirmations—Juvenile literature.
Classification: LCC BV4571.3 .F45 2021 (print) | LCC BV4571.3 (ebook) | DDC 242/.62—dc23
LC record available at https://lccn.loc.gov/2021009131
LC ebook record available at https://lccn.loc.gov/2021009132

Scripture quotations taken from The Holy Bible, New International Version®, NIV®. Copyright
© 1973, 1978, 1984, 2011 by Biblica, Inc.® Used by permission of Zondervan. All rights reserved
worldwide. www.Zondervan.com. The "NIV" and "New International Version" are trademarks
registered in the United States Patent and Trademark Office by Biblica, Inc.®

Author is represented by The Christopher Ferebee Agency, www.christopherferebee.com.

Zonderkidz is a trademark of Zondervan.

Zondervan titles may be purchased in bulk for educational, business, fundraising, or sales
promotional use. For information, please email SpecialMarkets@Zondervan.com.

Additional editorial services by Hungry Planet.

Cover Design: Micah Kandros
Interior Design: Denise Froehlich

Printed in Korea

---

21 22 23 24 25 SAM 10 9 8 7 6 5 4 3 2 1

CONTENTS

★ ★ ★ ★ ★

THE POWER OF DAILY
DECLARATIONS

★ ★ ★ ★ ★

Have you ever lied? Do you sometimes say things that aren't true just so people will like you or you won't get in trouble? Lying is something that most of us do from time to time, but each time that we do we get deeper and deeper into trouble. Unlike Pinocchio, our noses don't grow, but our relationships might just break.

The truth is we don't just lie to others, we sometimes lie to ourselves, and that can be just as bad as lying to someone else—if not worse. When we lie to ourselves we believe things that can make us worried and fearful. When we lie to ourselves, we build our dreams, hopes, and fears on something that isn't solid. It's like building your Jenga tower on an air mattress in the pool. It might stand up for a minute, but it won't last for long.

When I finally realized that I was building my life on a pile of lies, I decided to do something about it. So, I grabbed some paper and started to write down all the lies I'd been telling myself:

I'm scared of what might happen.
No one loves me.
I'll never get any better.
Why was I even born?

Looking at this list made me sad. I didn't want to be sad. And I didn't want to keep lying to myself. So I opened up the Bible and looked for the truth to confront my lies. What came out of that work was this book. I came up with 52 Daily Declarations that proved my lies wrong. Then I started to read these declarations for two minutes each morning. I read them out loud. And one by one I rejected the lies I had been telling myself were true when God was telling me they weren't. Three days later I felt totally different. I wasn't so stressed out or fearful. I wasn't as angry, and I wasn't as worried.

You might not believe that, but it's true! Taking two minutes each morning to recite these Daily Declarations changed my life. Now, whenever I start to freak out or feel bad for myself, I shut it down with the truth of who God is, what God says, and who I am as his child.

You might be thinking, *I don't lie to myself. I don't need Daily Declarations*. I hear you, but have a look at the table of contents and see if any of the lies you see listed there are something you, up until now, thought were true. Chances are you will find some lies you didn't even realize you were telling yourself.

So how does this work? I'm glad you asked. First, take a look at the Two-Minute Challenge. It would be best if you would read the Daily Declarations out loud to get them into your brain better. After reading those, read through the devotions at your own pace. Each of the fifty-two entries goes into the *what* and *why* behind the declarations. These are designed to help you better understand the lies you've been telling yourself and get to the truth of who you *really* are as a child of God.

All you will need besides this book is a pen and a friend or family member who wants to go through it with you. You can go through the book alone, but sometimes getting together with others helps you to see the truth better than when you are by yourself.

As a believer, you have the Spirit of Almighty God living inside of you. That means that you have access to all the power you need to stop the lies and embrace the truth.

So, if you're ready to break free from the lies that make you scared, stressed out, and worried, then you have everything you need, because God's power is in you!

Margaret

THE TWO-MINUTE DAILY CHALLENGE
DAILY POWER DECLARATIONS

★ ★ ★ ★ ★

So, are you up for the challenge?

Yes?

Then here it is: I dare you to take two minutes every day and read these Daily Declarations out loud for the next 30 days. All of them are rooted in Scripture, and you'll find this list on page 157 as well, with the Scripture references. You might like one particular statement more than another and want to repeat that one a few extra times. As you do, see if you can tell what the Holy Spirit brings to your mind as you read.

★ Jesus is King of my life.

★ I am who Christ says I am.

★ I take every thought captive. I smash every lie that enters my mind.

★ My purpose is to love, serve, glorify, and enjoy God forever.

★ I am filled with the Holy Spirit. The same power that raised Jesus from the dead lives in me.

★ I am God's kid and he thinks I'm wonderful. I am fearfully and wonderfully made, beautiful beyond measure.

* The power of God guards my thoughts, the Word of God guides my steps, and the favor of God rests on me.

* Worry is not the boss of me. I trust in the Lord with all my heart and I don't lean on my own understanding. In all my ways I will acknowledge him, and he will make my paths straight.

* The Lord is my shepherd. I don't need anything more than he's given me. He makes me lie down in green pastures. He leads me beside still waters. He restores my soul.

* God is my strength, my shield. He's always with me, always for me, always sees me. No weapon formed against me will prosper.

* I am anointed, empowered, and called to reach people who don't know God.

* My words have power. I will look for every opportunity to speak life, show compassion, and bring out the best in others.

* Shame is not my master. God's power is perfected in my weakness.

* I won't let unforgiveness control my life. I will forgive over and over because I am forgiven.

* I am an overcomer and ambassador. I refuse to listen to Satan or freak out when things don't go my way.

* God works all things together for my good and his glory.

* I will find God in every situation.

* I am on God's team today.

JESUS IS KING OF MY LIFE.

LIE: I'D BE HAPPY IF ONLY _____

★ ★ ★ ★ ★

You shall have no other gods before me.

EXODUS 20:3

When Moses, the leader of the Israelites, disappears up the side of a mountain, those left behind get worried. They start thinking maybe their leader has fallen off a cliff. The people run to Moses's brother Aaron and say they'll *be happy if only* they can have a god to lead them. So, they pile up everyone's gold earrings, melt them down, and forge a fancy cow sculpture. Then they throw a raging party and parade the golden beast all over camp.

Convinced God is too difficult to follow, they create a god they can lead wherever they want.

The Lord is fuming at their betrayal and by the time Moses

returns to camp with two stone tablets in his hands, he finds a wild party. Moses gets so upset he smashes the tablets and grinds the golden calf into powder, never to be seen or worshiped again. When Moses asked the people to choose, either you're for the Lord or you're not, God spared the lives of those that chose him.

Moses climbs the mountain a second time. He comes back with a couple of brand new tablets listing all the rules on idolatry. God says his people can't have other gods or make anything an idol (Exodus 20:3–4). In fact, he says if they make idols, they will be punished and so will their kids, and their kids, and their kids, and their kids (see Exodus 20:5). God's not messing around.

So what does all this talk about idols have to do with you? You don't have any idols, or do you? Here's how to find out. Fill in the blank:

I'D BE HAPPY IF ONLY _____.

Whatever you put in the blank is an idol.

When you need something more than God to make you happy, you create idols. Baby gods—those things you love so much and can't possibly live without—promise to save and complete you, but ultimately they crush you. They make you feel good until they make you need them so much you feel like you'd die without them. And you end up giving your heart to something you think will save you but ultimately destroys you.

> When you confess that Jesus is the only ruler of your life, you will find God's rescue from darkness.

The Lord has designed a better way for you to live. When

you confess that Jesus is the only ruler of your life, you will find God's rescue from darkness and enjoy a full and eternal life. The choice is yours.

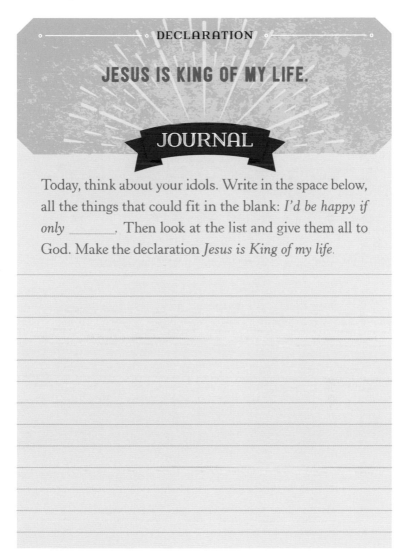

DECLARATION

JESUS IS KING OF MY LIFE.

JOURNAL

Today, think about your idols. Write in the space below, all the things that could fit in the blank: *I'd be happy if only* _____. Then look at the list and give them all to God. Make the declaration *Jesus is King of my life.*

I AM WHO CHRIST SAYS I AM.

LIE: I'M NOT ENOUGH.

★ ★ ★ ★ ★

*You are a chosen people, a royal priesthood, a
holy nation, God's special possession, that you
may declare the praises of him who called you
out of darkness into his wonderful light.*

1 PETER 2:9

In the beginning, God creates the world and he calls it good. Then
a dark character slithers into the scene and whispers twisted lies.
He says that God doesn't want Adam and Eve to know all that
he knows. That's why God's holding back the fruit (Genesis 3:4)
from the tree of the knowledge of good and evil from them. The
serpent creates separation between God and humans, and Eve
wants to be more than she is.

Seems dumb that Eve fell for it, but then how many times have I told myself that I'm not enough? As a kid I was so stressed out about it that I worked extra hard to prove to myself and everyone else that I *was* enough. In fact, I worked so hard that I gave myself an ulcer. Take that stomach! My 'not enoughness' led me to a life of anxiety, discontentment, and fear.

Maybe you have the feeling that you are not enough for your parents or your friends. Not enough for your teachers. Not even enough for God. Maybe you've been tempted to believe . . . *You are not smart enough. You are not attractive enough. You are not enough*_____. (You fill in the blank.)

This lie is so effective that Satan tries it on Jesus: "You say you're the Son of God? . . . then turn these stones into fresh baked loaves, leap from the top of the temple, kneel to me and have all the kingdoms of the world."

"You can't do it?"

"Then you're not enough!"

But Jesus knows better. He uses God's Word to prove that doing those things doesn't make him enough. *God* makes him enough (see Matthew 4:1–11). Scripture proves that Jesus is deeply loved, celebrated, and powerful. And so are you.

You can use the truths of Scripture to refute the lie that you are not enough. Remember that *you* are holy, chosen, an adopted child and heir of God. Remember that you are redeemed, forgiven, and chosen by God (Ephesians 1:1–8). You're showered with God's love—you aren't just his friend, you're family (1 John 3:1).

If Christ sits on the throne of your life, then he's the One who has the final say about who you are. Jesus sees you when others overlook you, he hears you when others ignore you, and he makes you more powerful than you imagine.

DECLARATION

I AM WHO CHRIST SAYS I AM.

JOURNAL

Today, journal about your feelings of being not enough. When have you felt not good enough? After you look at the negative thoughts in your life, look up Scripture that tells you who you are in Christ and make the declaration, "I am who Christ says I am."

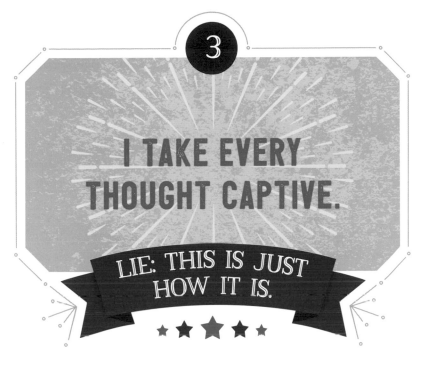

I TAKE EVERY THOUGHT CAPTIVE.

LIE: THIS IS JUST HOW IT IS.

★ ★ ★ ★ ★

We take captive every thought to make it
obedient to Christ.

2 CORINTHIANS 10:5B

When my friend Holden's new puppy died, I was sure my dog would be next. I was so scared. I freaked myself out about it. It was all I could think about. You've probably done the same. A group of friends have a party without you and suddenly you're thinking about all the reasons nobody likes you and you'll never be happy again. You analyze all that you could have done wrong and think about how horrible they are for not including you.

Psychologists call this "overthinking," which means losing control of your thoughts and obsessing over stuff. The more you worry, the more you feel anxious and discouraged. Your brain doesn't know the difference between reality and the stuff you are worried about. It all hurts just the same. And you ultimately become what you think.

Whatever you allow to control your mind determines your day. In fact, the more you think about something, the more your brain gets addicted to thinking that way. No wonder God is so committed to getting your attention back on him, and he has told you how in his Word. Second Corinthians 10:5 says you just take every thought captive, that means you don't let them have the run of your mind, but you stop them when you notice that they are negative.

> You ultimately become what you think.

After you've stopped the bad thoughts, you have to replace them with good thoughts. Say a prayer, speak a verse, give a compliment, say your Daily Declarations, breathe. As you do, you help your brain learn a new way of being.

Whenever you get into a spiral of negative thoughts, figure out what lie you are telling yourself by looking into God's Word for the truth and start to tell yourself that truth.

Talk to your parents, a Christian friend, or pastor about your negative thoughts, even if—like me—you're embarrassed to say them. It might be a little freaky to be so transparent, but you'll probably find out that you're not alone. And the Holy Spirit will work through them to help you stop the negative thoughts.

I TAKE EVERY THOUGHT CAPTIVE.

JOURNAL

What thoughts worry you? Write them here, then cross each one of them out as you declare, "I take every thought captive." Put your thoughts in jail. Draw chains on them, put bars around them. Doodle whatever you want that shows you are taking your thoughts captive.

4

I SMASH EVERY LIE THAT ENTERS MY MIND.

LIE: MY LIFE WILL NEVER GET BETTER.

We demolish arguments and every pretension that sets itself up against the knowledge of God.

2 CORINTHIANS 10:5A

What bad things do you think about yourself? These are probably things you say to yourself when you do something dumb, or when you don't like something about yourself. I actually have a lot of those thoughts. So one day when I had decided I was tired of those thoughts ruling my life, I shut myself in a room with paper and pen and I prayed. There, I scribbled a list of my lies:

- I am ugly.
- I am unlovable.

- I am unworthy of good things.
- I should be better than I am.

I cried as I realized I was locked in a dungeon of lies that left me alone, ashamed, afraid, trapped. Through constant repetition, these toxic thoughts had become something my mind believed was true. I believed a bunch of lies, and when you believe a lie over and over again, it becomes the truth to your body and mind.

One of the worst things to say to yourself is that your life will never get better. You'll never get taller or thinner. You'll never find someone who loves you, or get better grades. The more you think these negative thoughts the more they come true. You're like Nancy Drew, collecting clues that prove that your life is a total mess. And before you know it, your hopes and dreams are gone and you've given up your God-given destiny.

But it doesn't have to stay like this. You can smash those lies to pieces. The apostle Paul smashed lies and tore down walls built up to keep out the truth of God (see 2 Corinthians 10.5).

My psychologist friend, Curt Thompson, says most people who visit his office come because they have not been paying attention to what they are paying attention to. So let's start paying attention to what you pay attention to. What do you think about yourself? What do you say to yourself? Is it really true and is God saying the same thing? Remember, if the God who made the galaxies lives inside you, then you have the power—through Christ—to smash every destructive thought that raises itself up against the truth of

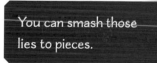
You can smash those lies to pieces.

God. Don't let your mind agree with the enemy. Agree with God and smash those lies.

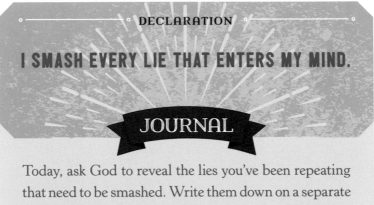

DECLARATION

I SMASH EVERY LIE THAT ENTERS MY MIND.

JOURNAL

Today, ask God to reveal the lies you've been repeating that need to be smashed. Write them down on a separate piece of paper. When you are done, smash the paper up in your hands as you say, "I smash the lies and tear down the walls I've built up to keep out the truth of God." Journal below about how that made you feel.

5

MY PURPOSE IS TO LOVE GOD.

MORE STUFF WILL MAKE ME HAPPY AND MAKE ME FEEL LOVED.

★ ★ ★ ★ ★

We love because he first loved us.

1 JOHN 4:19

When I was a girl, I loved stuffed animals. I had all the best stuffed animals, and I had tons of clothes for them, and every time we went shopping I wanted another stuffed animal. I can remember begging and pleading with my mom for one and my mom saying, "Not today, honey." I would whine and complain like a baby every time that happened. My life just wasn't full until I got the stuff I wanted.

You might not be dying for the latest Build a Bear, but maybe you feel like you can't be happy without the latest toy innovation.

And once you get it, you feel like life is finally perfect, at least for a while. When your friends come over, you are so excited to show them your newest purchase, and you just know they will be impressed!

The ads you see try to convince you that you have to have the newest thing in order to truly be happy, and it's easy to believe that's true. Your friends might even agree. But when you decide that stuff makes you happy, you become a consumer above all else. You start thinking everything that God says he will be to you can be gotten at the store. You start to tell yourself, "If I can just get_____, then I'll feel better." We all fall for this lie too many times to count.

But maybe you've noticed that the stuff you get and love so much only makes you happy for a little while, then like Woody in *Toy Story*, it gets replaced by your new favorite Buzz Lightyear or some other new must-have toy. Stuff loses its excitement, it loses its ability to make you happy because it will never love you back. But there is One who does love you back. In fact, he doesn't just love you back, he loved you *first*. You're actually the one loving him back.

> Only God's love can make you happy, no matter what you own.

Only God's love can make you happy. Did you know that you were created to love God with all your heart and soul? Until he becomes your everything, you will keep trying to find happiness in stuff. But maybe you don't know how to love God like that. Stuff is easier because you can see it and touch it. God seems so distant. But what you have to know is that God loved you before you even knew him. He's not distant, he's right here, just waiting for you to love him back.

MY PURPOSE IS TO LOVE GOD.

JOURNAL

Today, write down all the stuff that you love but *could* live without. After that, write down the declaration: *My purpose is to love God,* and underline it.

Below these words, write down all the stuff you love but feel like you *can't* live without. Take a look at this list and tell yourself, *My purpose is to love God.* Think about how God will be your comfort and your protection even if you didn't have those things anymore.

6

MY PURPOSE IS TO SERVE GOD.

LIE: I'M TOO YOUNG TO HAVE A MINISTRY.

★ ★ ★ ★ ★

For in him we live and move and have our being.

ACTS 17:28

So how do you feel when you think about becoming a teenager? Are you excited to babysit? To drive a car? To get a job? Or are you scared thinking about growing up? I mean it's fun being a kid, who wants to stop that, right?

I remember when I was your age. I was not interested in growing up. I liked my collection of teddy bears and my toys. I wasn't in a hurry to have responsibilities. I also remember being taught in church that it was important to serve God, but it didn't seem like there were as many opportunities as there were for adults. So how can kids serve God?

Do you know what Jesus said was the sum of all of the commandments? The most important commandment in all the Bible? He said it was to love God and to love your neighbor as yourself (see Matthew 22:36–40). So knowing that that is God's number one goal for his people, how do you think it affects your ministry? Can you do that kind of ministry? Can you love others? If you can do that—if you can love the kids who are picked last for dodge ball or who sit alone at lunch. If you can love the kid who took the seat you wanted, or who doesn't always come to school clean and dressed well, then you have a ministry of loving others.

> Loving others means thinking of them the way God thinks of them.

Loving others is all about thinking of them the way God thinks of them—as his children. How can you ignore God's child? How can you be mean to someone who God created in his image? When you think about it like that, having a ministry is something you can have at any age.

You might be too young to vote or drive, but you are never too young to care about people who are lonely, left out, or lacking love. Look around you today. See who needs a friend and tell yourself, "I was made for this!" The kindness you share today may become an opportunity to share the grace of God with a new friend. And loving others the way God loves turns everyone into a friend.

MY PURPOSE IS TO SERVE GOD.

JOURNAL

Today, think about all the people you see during your day who may be left out. Write down their names or a description of them, if you don't know their names yet. Then write down five things you could do that would be nice for them. It could be as easy as asking them how they are or what their name is. It could be sitting with them at lunch or bringing them into your group. Whatever it is, your ministry awaits!

MY PURPOSE IS TO GLORIFY GOD.

LIE: THEY ARE TOO MEAN TO BE KIND TO.

★ ★ ★ ★ ★

Do nothing out of selfish ambition or vain conceit,
Rather in humility value others above yourselves.

PHILIPPIANS 2:3

I bet if I asked you to give me a list of your sins you'd have a hard time thinking of any, wouldn't you? I know when I was a kid, sin was the last thing on my mind. And after all, how much can a little kid sin?

The Old Testament says sin is rebellion against God. The New Testament calls it 'missing the mark.' That means it's like shooting an arrow that misses the bullseye and lands in your pool float instead. Sin isn't just the obvious stuff like stealing and lying, it's missing the mark of being loving by thinking about yourself instead of others (see Philippians 2:3).

So think about it like this: What did you do the last time your brother or sister took something that was yours? Did you tell on them? Did you hit them or ruin something of theirs? That might not seem like sin, but when you care more about you and your stuff than loving others, that's sin. It's called selfishness.

Sin isn't just the stuff you read about in the ten commandments. There is more to it than that. You probably know it is a sin to kill someone, but did you know that it's a sin to even call your brother a fool (see Matthew 5:21–26). See, sin isn't just the stuff you do, it's how you think about people, and thinking mean thoughts about people is as bad as doing mean things to them.

I know that it's really hard to stop thinking about yourself. I mean, you are with yourself 24 hours a day. But God gives you the power to change the subject from yourself to others.

> God gives you the power to change the subject from yourself to others.

Humility is thinking less about yourself and trusting God to be the one who will protect and defend you. When you act in humility and trust God it's a lot easier to love others. The fight isn't yours. The prayer is yours. So the next time your brother comes into your room uninvited, rely on the power of God to love him and not to throw something at him. And when you get in trouble for doing something, trust God to defend you in the eyes of those who are mad at you. You don't have to fight, he will fight for you. He is your defender. All you have to do is think as much about others as you do about yourself.

MY PURPOSE IS TO GLORIFY GOD.

JOURNAL

This week, make a list of things that you think are unacceptable—like coming into your room uninvited or using your toys without asking. Think of all the things that make you angry or that start fights with family or friends. Then pray over each of those things. Ask God to help you have the power to be kind when you are often mean.

8

MY PURPOSE IS TO ENJOY GOD FOREVER.

LIE: GOD PUTS UP WITH ME.

★ ★ ★ ★ ★

Take delight in the LORD.

PSALM 37:4

Have you ever felt like you're not doing enough for God? Maybe deep inside you think you don't . . .

pray enough.
read your Bible enough.
share your faith enough.
change the world enough.

The enemy loves it when you think you aren't doing enough for God. He wants you to think God is too hard to please so that you will give up trying. He wants you to think that God doesn't really love you; he just puts up with you.

But from the beginning God wanted only one thing from you: He wanted *you.*

God cares about you more than you care about you. He adores you so much that he sent his only son Jesus to die for you (Romans 5:8). When God looks at you, he sings, dances, and shouts for joy (Zephaniah 3:17). Oh, how God values you!

> From the beginning God wanted only one thing from you: He wanted *you.*

And oh, how he wants you to love him. One of the ways you can do that is by thinking about him. Think of his power and kindness. We call this "quiet time," a part of the day when you pause the rest of life and sit alone with your Father.

In his presence is where you belong. It's where you are the most yourself.

So how do you find God? Deuteronomy 4:29 says, "You will find him if you seek him with all your heart and with all your soul." Your mind might wander to other things, but the longer you can come back to his presence, the more you will experience him in new ways.

As you spend time in the quiet, ask God what he's trying to tell you. Then see what comes to mind. Sometimes it might be a friend who needs your prayers. Sometimes it might be a family member or even a stranger. And sometimes he just wants to talk about you.

So the next time you pray, instead of just listing all the people and things you want to pray for, stop and listen. Ask God what he wants to tell you. Don't give up after a couple seconds. Wait and keep bringing your mind back to him.

When you start to think that God doesn't value you, that he just tolerates you, remind yourself that is a total lie. You know the truth. God is madly in love with you and he values you as his child.

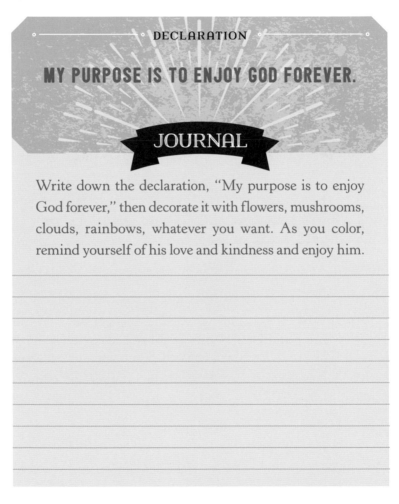

DECLARATION

MY PURPOSE IS TO ENJOY GOD FOREVER.

JOURNAL

Write down the declaration, "My purpose is to enjoy God forever," then decorate it with flowers, mushrooms, clouds, rainbows, whatever you want. As you color, remind yourself of his love and kindness and enjoy him.

9

I AM FILLED WITH THE HOLY SPIRIT.

LIE: I HAVE TO DO IT ON MY OWN.

★ ★ ★ ★ ★

The Advocate, the Holy Spirit, whom the Father
will send in my name, will teach you all things and
will remind you of everything I have said to you.

JOHN 14:26

What do you do when you get lonely? Do you call a friend? Watch TV? Cry? Being lonely can be a tough thing, and most of us want to do all we can to not feel alone. But for the Christian, loneliness has an answer. When Jesus left earth, he said he would send us an advocate, a helper, to be with us so that we would never be alone. This helper is called the Holy Spirit, and he enters the life of every believer and never leaves.

Jesus sent the Holy Spirit so you would never have to do life alone. When you decide to become a follower of Jesus, he stays with you all of the time. He is your constant companion and he gives you access to his power.

> When you just can't do it by yourself, the Holy Spirit
>   helps you.
> When you're hurting, the Holy Spirit comforts you.
> When you feel lost, the Holy Spirit shows you the way.
> When you can't find the words to pray, the Holy Spirit
>   prays for you.
> When you're scared of making the wrong decision, the
>   Holy Spirit counsels you.
> When you feel weak, the Holy Spirit strengthens you.

The Holy Spirit also lets you know when you're making a bad choice, so you won't fall into sin. He is the one who changes you into the image of Christ (2 Corinthians 3:18), and teaches you the deep things of God (1 Corinthians 2:10). The Spirit isn't an accessory to your life, but the doorway to all that Christ has for you.

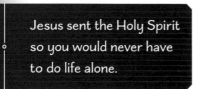

Jesus sent the Holy Spirit so you would never have to do life alone.

The Spirit works through you to help others. He's your constant companion.

When you have the Holy Spirit, you have the Spirit of God living inside of you. His power is always with you, but when you forget about him, you miss out on the power within. The Holy Spirit isn't talked about much, but he is just as much God as the Father and the Son. He is with you—leading you, guiding you, strengthening you, and empowering you. You can lean on him every minute of every day, especially when you feel lonely.

But how do you lean on him? You lean on him through prayer, through Bible reading, and through taking daily time to just be quiet and listen, and to wait on him.

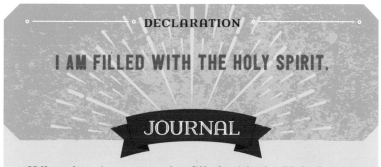

What does it mean to be filled with the Holy Spirit? Below, draw a design like a house or a heart or something with a big space in the middle. Then write all the things the Holy Spirit is to you, for example a counselor, comfort, teacher, etc.

10

THE SAME POWER THAT RAISED JESUS FROM THE DEAD LIVES IN ME.

LIE: I'LL NEVER RECOVER FROM THIS.

★ ★ ★ ★ ★

And if the Spirit of him who raised Jesus from the dead is living in you . . .

ROMANS 8:11

Have you ever heard the story of Dr. Frankenstein and his monster? You've probably seen costumes of the green-faced monster at Halloween time, trick or treating from house to house. But Frankenstein was infamous for bringing his monster back from the dead. The story isn't real, obviously, how could it be since no one can bring anyone or anything back to life. But that's exactly what God did when Jesus died on the cross, he brought Jesus back to life. We call this miracle, that only God can do, the resurrection. Jesus was resurrected from the dead.

Think about what it must mean to raise someone from the dead. It would take all the power in the world to do it: All the power that only God, as the all-powerful, most powerful, being in the universe could do. This display of his strength is important to you as a Christian because when Jesus was resurrected, he won the battle with death. He defeated it. And that's important because that means that death no longer has control of you. You don't have to be afraid of it. But, it also means something else. If the all-powerful God of the universe can bring Jesus back to life, he can bring you through every tough circumstance that you could ever face.

When your life gets out of control and you feel like things will never get better. When you can't see an end to your suffering . . . remember that your God can bring a dead man back to life, so surely he can bring you through the tough circumstances of life.

If your best friend betrays you, or your family has to move across the country taking you away from everything and everyone you know, God can bring you through it because the same power that raised Jesus from the dead lives in you. If you fail a test and are grounded for a week, God can bring you through that too.

> The resurrection power that raised Jesus from the dead lives in you.

The resurrection power that raised Jesus from the dead lives in you. God can heal you. No evil is too powerful for him to overcome. No sin is so stubborn that he cannot forgive. Allow God to raise you up into the light of his healing.

THE SAME POWER THAT RAISED JESUS FROM THE DEAD LIVES IN ME.

JOURNAL

What things in your life seem too big for you to handle? Maybe you have a big test coming up or a friend who is mad at you. Whatever it is, journal about it today. Then remind yourself that *the same power that resurrected Christ from the dead lives in you.* Write that in big letters at the end of your journaling.

11

I AM GOD'S KID AND HE THINKS I'M WONDERFUL.

LIE: I'LL NEVER BE GOOD ENOUGH.

★ ★ ★ ★ ★

"This is my Son, whom I love; with him I am well pleased."

MATTHEW 3:17

We are all storytellers, sometimes we just keep our stories to ourselves. The stories you tell yourself can come from all kinds of places—from your parents, your siblings, your friends, your enemies. The stories you tell yourself might make you feel better or they might make you feel worse. One of the worst stories I ever told myself was, "You'll never amount to anything." I got this story from my sixth grade teacher, Mrs. Smith.

I was a hyperactive kid. I was always distracted and probably ate more sugar than I should have. So I totally understand why

Mrs. Smith would be frustrated with me back then. But I bet she never realized that her frustration would be the story of my life for a very, very long time.

I really don't remember any other words Mrs. Smith spoke to me that year, but I just can't forget those. They stung deep inside of me and fed my deepest childhood insecurities. From that moment on, I was convinced that I would truly never be good enough.

The lie "I'll never be good enough" sounds a lot like "I'll never be enough" doesn't it? They are really close, they just have different results. Never-good-enough makes you work so hard you're miserable, and never-enough makes you just wanna give up. Both are bad.

So what's the truth? That you are good enough, smart enough, and that people like you? Sure, some of that might be true, but deep inside you will always see failures and fear rejection. That's why it's important to understand that the real truth is that you *will* never be good enough. Wait, what? That's right, because only God's good work in you will be enough. He is the only perfect one, the only one who can save you from your failure and their rejection.

> You are *in Christ* and that means you get all the benefits he offers, including his fierce love for you and his favor.

Imagine if every day you knew that you were good enough because of Jesus. Imagine how you wouldn't have to worry about being a failure because God works all things, even your failure, together for the good of those who love him. As a Christian, you are *in Christ* and that means you get all the benefits he offers, including his fierce love for you and his favor.

I AM GOD'S KID AND HE THINKS I'M WONDERFUL.

JOURNAL

Write down three ways in which God has made you wonderful.

_____

_____

_____

_____

_____

_____

_____

_____

_____

_____

_____

_____

_____

_____

_____

_____

_____

_____

_____

_____

_____

_____

I AM FEARFULLY AND WONDERFULLY MADE.

LIE: I'M SO UGLY.

★ ★ ★ ★ ★

I praise you because I am fearfully and
wonderfully made; your works are wonderful, I
know that full well.

PSALM 139:14

Do you love every inch of yourself? Do you like your nose, your
hair, your body? Your personality? When I was nine years old I
was totally happy with myself until one of the kids in my class
said something mean about my size. I didn't even know I was that
much bigger than anyone else until she said that, and suddenly I
was ashamed of my body. So that no one would stare at my body,
I never let anyone stand behind me. I tucked myself toward the
back of every line. I was just so embarrassed.

When we start to compare ourselves to others, we start to judge ourselves, and when we judge ourselves as less good than someone else, it starts a pattern of negative thoughts—*You're not smart enough. You're not good looking enough. You weigh too much.* Maybe when *you* look in the mirror, you feel shame or turn away in disgust.

The trouble with all of this negative self-talk is that it doesn't just stop with your looks and your brains. It sometimes spreads over to how you feel about your soul. If your outside is ugly, then your inside must be ugly too. When you start to think like that, you can start to feel like no one could ever love you. You might start to feel isolated and alone, too ugly or stupid for anyone to spend time with. If you've ever felt like that, let me tell you a little secret: You, my dear friend, were made in the image of God. You are the object of his love. He made you just the way you are for a very special reason. You are his child, his own. You are fearfully and wonderfully made. **You are embedded with wonder upon wonder.** What makes you so beautiful? The glory of Christ living in *you.* Our infinite God created you to show his glory to the world. When you say, "I'm not good looking enough, or smart enough, or anything enough," you point a finger at God and say, "You are not as good an artist as you think you are."

The secret to breaking free from this negative self-talk is tucked into today's verse. So remember you are fearfully and wonderfully made. Praise God for that today. Thank him for every physical inch of you. Praise him every day. As God's child, you are beautiful beyond measure and a one-of-a-kind masterpiece.

> You are fearfully and wonderfully made.

I AM FEARFULLY AND WONDERFULLY MADE.

JOURNAL

Today, write down everything you can think of to thank God for. Thank him for your hair, your face, your skin, your size. Thank him for everything that he made you to be.

13

I AM BEAUTIFUL BEYOND MEASURE.

I'M TOO YOUNG TO SHINE JESUS.

★ ★ ★ ★ ★

Don't let anyone look down on you because you
are young, but set an example for the believers in
speech, in conduct, in love, in faith and in purity.

1 TIMOTHY 4:12

A lot of kids can't wait to grow up. They want to do all the things that older kids do. They want freedom and more responsibility. They want to be more than they are today, and they want to be considered important. Sometimes being the youngest means that everyone thinks you don't know anything, but that doesn't have to be the case. There are stories of boys and girls throughout history who have changed the world.

The Apostle Paul was discipling Timothy. Timothy was a

spiritual son to him. He was serving God and moving into ministry in the footsteps of his mentor, but he still struggled with people not taking him seriously. That's why we see Paul writing to him in the book 1 Timothy saying, "Don't let anyone look down on you because you are young, but set an example for the believers in speech, in conduct, in love, in faith and in purity."

Paul wants to make sure that Timothy doesn't think because he is young he cannot serve God. It is important to respect older people and recognize that they might know more than you, but that doesn't mean you are not an example in the way you talk and act. When you love others well. When you show your faith by being faithful to God and loving him with all your heart, soul, mind, and strength, you affect the people around you for Christ.

There is never a time when you are too young to be an ambassador for God. There is never a time when people don't need to know that kids can have a relationship

> When you show your faith by being faithful to God and loving him with all your heart, soul, mind, and strength you affect the people around you for Christ.

with Christ. The fact that you have faith in Jesus means that you are meant for a great purpose, and that purpose will always include telling others about Jesus.

People might continue to think that you are too young to know anything about God, but knowing God doesn't have anything to do with how old you are. It has to do with how much you have surrendered your life to God. Trust that once you turn over your life to him he will begin to use you for his kingdom.

I AM BEAUTIFUL BEYOND MEASURE.

JOURNAL

Today, ask God to show you who around you is watching to see how you live your faith. Do you have a smaller sibling, neighbor, or friend? Do you have family members who are watching you to see if you really believe what you say you believe? Write down the names that come to mind and start to pray for them. Pray they would hear from God, know him, and surrender their lives to him. Pray for them every day this week and beyond.

THE POWER OF GOD GUARDS MY THOUGHTS.

LIE: THE WORLD IS FULL OF SCARY THINGS.

★ ★ ★ ★ ★

Whatever is true, whatever is noble, whatever
is right, whatever is pure, whatever is lovely,
whatever is admirable—if anything is excellent
or praiseworthy—think about such things.

PHILIPPIANS 4:8

Have you ever been told a lie by someone and believed it? How does it make you feel when you fall for a lie? Not so great, huh? Lies can hurt, make you feel dumb for believing them, and even make you do crazy stuff. It is far better to know the right thing to do and to do it. It is the lovely things, the admirable things, the excellent things in life that build up instead of tear down.

But a lot of times you look around and all you see is bad stuff, ugly stuff, lies. That's how it was for the Apostle Paul. He lived through a lot of really bad and unlovely stuff—imprisonment, shipwrecks, ridicule. But Paul didn't concentrate on the bad stuff. He focused on the goodness of God. In the letter he wrote to the Philippian church, Paul told them how to see light on the darkest of days:

"Finally, brothers and sisters, whatever is true, whatever is noble, whatever is right, whatever is pure, whatever is lovely, whatever is admirable—if anything is excellent or praiseworthy—think about such things" (Philippians 4:8).

See, the secret to surviving all the scary stuff that's happening *around* you is discovering God's power *in* you.

> The secret to surviving all the scary stuff that's happening *around* you is discovering God's power *in* you.

Don't let anybody tell you that there is no hope, because our hope is in God, and God is in control. In the midst of all the chaos, a God of order is in charge. Just because circumstances are scary doesn't mean God isn't up to something good.

The Apostle Paul helps you overcome that feeling of hopelessness. This passage turned prayer empowers you to live with hope. Pray this right now:

Jesus, help me to see:

Whatever is true: Open my eyes to see truth when I'm afraid, worried, or stressed out.

Whatever is noble: Open my heart to see you, your character and presence, your power and your love.

Whatever is right: Open my mind to know how to discern right from wrong.

Whatever is pure: Open my will to your will.

Whatever is lovely: Open my ears so that I can hear your words, recognize your actions, and sense your presence in me and around me.

Whatever is admirable: Open my mouth to speak words that are respectful, kind, and patient. Amen.

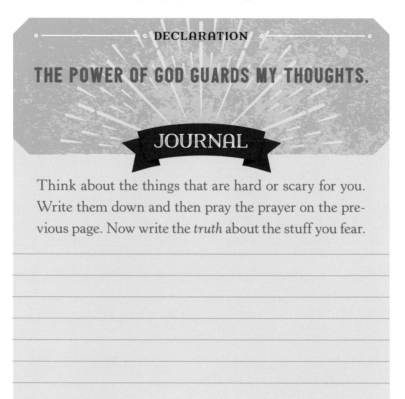

--- ○ DECLARATION ○ ---

THE POWER OF GOD GUARDS MY THOUGHTS.

JOURNAL

Think about the things that are hard or scary for you. Write them down and then pray the prayer on the previous page. Now write the *truth* about the stuff you fear.

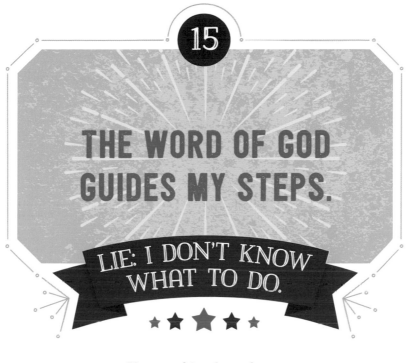

15

THE WORD OF GOD GUIDES MY STEPS.

LIE: I DON'T KNOW WHAT TO DO.

★ ★ ★ ★ ★

Your word is a lamp for my feet, a light on my path.

PSALM 119:105

When I was 11 years old, my best friend really wanted me to show her the answers on a test we were taking. She kept pushing me to do it. I knew that if I didn't she would fail and I really didn't want her to fail, so I let her look at my paper. I figured it was the kind thing to do—help a friend. But after we got our tests back, the teacher wanted to talk to us. It wasn't good news. She could tell we cheated because we had had different tests. So it was obvious that my friend answered my test and not hers. Needless to say, I was grounded for that.

When it comes to making decisions about something you have a good idea isn't right to do, it's important you have a place to go, someone to ask. But if you are in a situation similar to mine, and there's not time to ask anyone, it's super important to have some idea what you'll do before you end up there. Did you know that God's Word has an answer for all of your questions? It does, but waiting until you are in the middle of a situation to look it up is a little too late. That's why it's so important to read your Bible every day, and to learn what pleases God.

Psalm 119:105 says, "Thy word is a lamp for my feet, and a light on my path." And that's a pretty good place to start. This means that if you have even a hint that God would not be pleased, in other words, you don't have faith that what you are doing is holy, then just don't do it. It's a simple fix. You may not know what is next, but with Christ, the Word, as your guide you always know what to do next.

> You may not know what is next, but with Christ, the Word, you always know what to do next.

God's Word will lead you, guide you, sustain you. Your friends and parents might speak words that encourage you, but God's Word will speak words that empower you and help you to make decisions that are faithful. Even if those decisions are hard and you know that making them will make your friends unhappy, knowing that it will please God makes those hard decisions a lot easier to make.

THE WORD OF GOD GUIDES MY STEPS.

JOURNAL

Today, get out your Bible and see if it has a concordance in the back. The concordance is a list of topics like love, forgiveness, hope, fights, etc. and it tells you where they are in the Bible. Look up a few things that interest you, like maybe anger, decisions, or protection. Pick out a few verses that you like. Write them here in your journal. Think about them, and ask God to help you make good decisions as you keep his Word in your heart.

THE FAVOR OF GOD RESTS ON ME.

LIE: IF I CHOOSE THE WRONG THING, I MIGHT RUIN EVERYTHING.

★ ★ ★ ★ ★

A person may plan his own journey, but the LORD directs his steps.

PROVERBS 16:9 (GW)

Sometimes I just can't make a decision. I worry about choosing the wrong thing, and so it can take me forever just to make up my mind. It's frustrating to me and to everyone else who is yelling at me to hurry up and make up my mind.

When I was your age, I was scared that if I chose the wrong thing it would be terrible. I would end up hating what I picked, someone else would get something better, or worse yet whatever

I chose would ruin the big plans God has for me. A lot of times making decisions is hard because you fear making a mistake. There were a lot of mistakes made in the Bible. There were a lot of famous men and women who did things they shouldn't have done. But God used all of those mistakes to advance his plans. In other words, people made the choices, but the Lord directed their steps.

You've probably heard the story of Jonah. Boy, did he make a bad decision. He was told to go to Nineveh to tell the people there about God's love for them, but he hated them so much he wouldn't do it. Of course, even that colossal decision to run away from God didn't change God's plan. In the end, Jonah went to Nineveh, and we have an amazing story of God's power over not only human choices, but the weather and the ocean.

In Psalm 139 it says, "Where can I go [to get away] from your Spirit? Where can I run [to get away] from you? If I go up to heaven, you are there. If I make my bed in hell, you are there. If I climb upward on the rays of the morning sun [or] land on the most distant shore of the sea where the sun sets, even there your hand would guide me and your right hand would hold on to me." (Psalm 139:7–10, GW) See, there's no way around it; God is everywhere.

> There's no way around it: God is everywhere.

Making decisions is always hard, and you don't have to rush it. But if you are worrying that a wrong decision might remove the favor of God from you, don't stress about it. If God has a plan for your life, he will redirect your steps to fulfill those plans.

THE FAVOR OF GOD RESTS ON ME.

JOURNAL

Have you made bad choices? Are there mistakes you've made that you fear have messed things up? Do you have a choice you need to make today? Today, write your thoughts to God. Tell him your fears and worries and then remind yourself that he will direct your steps.

WORRY IS NOT THE BOSS OF ME.

LIE: I CAN'T STOP WORRYING.

Therefore I tell you, do not worry about your life.

MATTHEW 6:25

How do you like taking tests? Do you ever get a little stressed out by the idea? Did you know that when you stress you actually drain your body of the energy you need to think clearly and remember the facts you've been learning? Stress isn't a helpful emotion at any time, but definitely not when you have to take a test. Turns out, the hormones that your body makes when you are stressed have been proven to contribute to memory loss. So don't stress the test!

Jesus tells us over and over again not to worry and teaches that worry is a taker, never a giver. In fact, he says, it won't even add a single hour to your life, but it might steal a few (see Matthew 6:27).

So what do you do when stress starts to tell you what to do? The answer might be simpler than you think. In Philippians 4:6 it says that in every situation, instead of giving into the worry, you should pray, but not just pray. You should thank God for all he's given you, make your requests known to him, and even beg him for what you need.

When a Christian prays, great things happen. Just think about it, every prayer itself is a miracle. After all, you are communicating with the God of the universe, Creator of all, and yet nothing you could pray to the all-powerful one is too insignificant, and nothing you could ask is too huge. God cares for all the things that matter to you.

> When a Christian prays, great things happen.

Did you know that prayer also opens you up to being used by God? That's because with prayer you get new eyes, freed from worry and open to see what God is doing in and around you.

It's really a good trade. In exchange for your anxious prayers you get peace. And not just any ordinary kind of peace, but peace that makes no sense since circumstances aren't peaceful. When you get the peace of God that makes no sense to the world, you stop the cycle of stress that can easily freak you out and make you unable to do the simplest thing.

The truth is that stressful stuff will always pop up in your life. Tests will need to be taken. Speeches will have to be given. But when they come, you aren't alone. God is with you. So pray, give thanks, and accept God's peace.

WORRY IS NOT THE BOSS OF ME.

JOURNAL

On this page, draw a big trash can. Inside of it, write all of the things you worry about. After you've done that, write the word 'prayer' below it. Then under that write a list of all the things you are thankful for. You can thank God and ask him to show himself to be bigger than all of your fears.

18

I TRUST IN THE LORD WITH ALL MY HEART.

LIE: I NEED TO BE IN CONTROL.

Trust in the LORD with all your heart.

PROVERBS 3:5

Have you ever wished you could make people do whatever you wanted them to do? Like when your brother or sister keeps taking your stuff or coming into your room uninvited, do you ever wish you had the power to make them obey your every word? Imagine what that kind of control would be like. If only everyone would treat you the way you want to be treated, give you what you want when you want it, and leave you alone when you want to be left alone—imagine how great life would be.

The truth is we all want that kind of life: a life of control. But controlling others is a waste of your time. In case you haven't figured it out, you can't do it. Sure, you can fight with them or tell on them, but you cannot change them. The trouble is, most of us tell ourselves if only we could get what we want, we would be happy—so that's all we focus on. And in the end we just end up mad.

The trouble with trying to control everything in your life so it turns out just how you want it is that you end up totally stressed out. But wait, there's more! It also makes everyone around you either mad at you or miserable. The truth is that whenever you try to control what you can't, you lose control of the one thing that you can: yourself.

> Whenever you try to control what you can't, you lose control of the one thing that you can: yourself.

The Bible has a word for your condition of control. It's called idolatry. That just means that you are trusting something or someone other than God to save, satisfy, or rule your future. Every time you reach for the joystick of control, you are telling God that he's not good at his job and he needs your help. And let me ask a question, how is the job of God going for you? Is your brother obeying you? Can you stop your sister from taking your stuff? Do your parents do whatever you ask? The truth is you will never be able to control the people in your life, and it isn't your job anyway.

All the stress you feel about your lack of control won't be fixed by getting control, but by turning over control to God. Every morning when you wake, tell God he can be God today, and whatever happens look to him as the one in control. Trust him even when you don't like what's happening and do what he's called you to do—love your enemies and do good to those who hate you.

I TRUST IN THE LORD WITH ALL MY HEART.

JOURNAL

Take some time and write a prayer to God, telling him you are ready for him to be in control. Be sure to thank him for all he does for you.

19

I WILL NOT LEAN ON MY UNDERSTANDING.

LIE: I HAVE TO TAKE CARE OF EVERYONE.

★ ★ ★ ★ ★

Do not lean on your own understanding.

PROVERBS 3:5 (NASB)

When I was younger, I thought that I had to take care of everyone. I had to keep serving, keep sacrificing, keep going until I had nothing left to give. I tried to be everything to everyone. If I collapsed into bed exhausted, I thought it was a good day. I thought I had to take care of the world to keep it moving.

Then I read a book called *Boundaries for Teens,* by John Townsend. I had no idea that my thoughts about saving the world were actually about me thinking I was God. I took on all the responsibility around me as if I were in charge of the world, like God really is. But then I realized that Jesus is the only one capable of being the

Savior of the world. I was leaning on my own understanding instead of God's understanding of how things are meant to work.

It's easy to believe the lie that you need to be the savior of your family and friends. You aren't being bad, or trying to tell God he isn't good enough. You just want to help. Believe me, I know.

But maybe the idea that you have to do it all comes from the fear that God *won't* do it all. You might think if you don't help or don't fix a situation, then no one will. You might think that your parents won't do it, or your friends or your siblings won't do it, but what you are really thinking is that God has left the building. He's no longer there and no longer taking care of you.

> Jesus is the only one capable of being the Savior of the world.

Whenever you think that you have to save everyone, fix everyone, or become the parent to your siblings or even your parents, you are forgetting that you are not the savior of the world. Jesus is the Savior.

Do you worry about your parents?
Do you think you are the only one who can fix things
     at home?
Do you wrestle with thoughts of fear?

If you answered yes to any of those or you feel something similar, then it's time to let go and let God be God. You are not the Messiah. You are not the savior of the world. The Savior's name is Jesus. And because of him, you don't have to stress to save the world. He's already done it for you.

I WILL NOT LEAN ON MY UNDERSTANDING.

JOURNAL

List 5 things you think you are responsible for, then go ask your parents if it's true.

IN ALL MY WAYS I WILL ACKNOWLEDGE HIM.

LIE: I'M TOO BUSY TO PRAY.

In all your ways acknowledge Him.

PROVERBS 3:6 (NASB)

When Philip first meets Jesus he is beyond excited. He is so excited that he runs to his friend Nathanael to tell him the good news (see John 1:45). But Nathanael is totally unimpressed. In fact, he asks if anything good can possibly come from Nazareth (John 1:46). Philip delivers an incredible gift—an invitation to meet the long-awaited Messiah—and Nathanael responds with a big ole' "nope."

But Philip doesn't give up. He throws in a few more choice words: "Come and see." And so Nate went and saw, and that's when it happened. Nate went from naysayer to yaysayer (John 1:49).

Have you become a yaysayer? Do you say yay to God or naw? Each morning you wake up you have the chance to say, "Yay, God, let's do this!" or, "Naw, not today God."

When I wake up each morning I say, "Holy Spirit, what do you want me to do today?" Then I sit, wait, and listen. Sometimes God reminds me to talk to a friend I've neglected, or to practice being quiet and talking less. Most of the time I find that what he wants me to do is to reach out to other people who might feel lonely or scared, and amazingly, reaching out to them helps me not to be so scared myself.

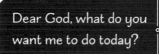

Dear God, what do you want me to do today?

I have a one-question prayer that you can try. It's so easy, you'll never forget it. It goes like this: "Dear God, what do you want me to do today?"

Are you willing to ask that question knowing that God might ask you to do something a little scary? Like talk to a new kid at school or ask a friend for forgiveness for something that you did? Are you willing to hear God out and do whatever he might bring into your mind?

Each and every day, when you wake up, you are invited to leap out of bed to "Come and see!" as if Christ has just moved to town and wants to lead you on a grand adventure. When you live your faith this way, it's never boring, and you never wonder if you are doing enough or if God is working through you. The more you ask him what he wants, the more he will show you and the more you will experience the presence of God.

IN ALL MY WAYS I WILL ACKNOWLEDGE HIM.

JOURNAL

Are you willing to ask God what he wants you to do today? Take some time right now and pray. Ask him what he wants you to do with your friends and family. As you sit in silence and think about who he is, how he loves, shows mercy, forgives, and serves, think of who he might be bringing to mind . . . who you need to reach out to today. As you think of them, write down their names, pray for them, and then plan to talk to them.

21

AND HE WILL MAKE MY PATHS STRAIGHT.

I'LL NEVER KNOW WHAT TO DO.

★ ★ ★ ★ ★

He will make your paths straight.

PROVERBS 3:6 (NASB)

Sometimes I have felt like God just wasn't listening. I would talk and cry and pray and get nothing in return. I felt so alone that it seemed like not even God was there. It was the worst feeling in the world. Some people say they hear God, or God speaks to them. They feel his presence, but I felt nothing. It made me think there was something wrong with me. Maybe I wasn't saved. If I was, why didn't I feel what others felt?

But then I read Luke 11:9, where Jesus was talking to his disciples who were asking him how to pray. The first part of his answer was what we call the Lord's Prayer, and it goes like this:

"'Father, hallowed be your name, your kingdom come. Give us each day our daily bread. Forgive us our sins, for we also forgive everyone who sins against us. And lead us not into temptation'" (Luke 11:2–4).

After he gave them that prayer to show them how to pray, he told the disciples this very important thing: "Which of you fathers, if your son asks for a fish, will give him a snake instead? Or if he asks for an egg, will give him a scorpion? If you then, though you are evil, know how to give good gifts to your children, how much more will your Father in heaven give the Holy Spirit to those who ask him!" (Luke 11:9–13)

These words made me think: If God is my Father, and good fathers don't give their kids something awful when they ask for something good that they need, why would I worry that God hasn't saved me? Why would I worry that because I didn't hear him he wasn't there? No, Jesus made it clear that if you look for him with all your heart, you will find him. It's Jesus' guarantee. If you ask God to be with you, he won't run away or hide from you. He is a good father. And if you're not sure what to do next, he will lead you, guide you, and make your paths straight (Proverbs 3:5).

> If you look for him with all your heart, you will find him. It's Jesus' guarantee.

If you feel like God just isn't there, like you just can't hear him, then look where he's speaking, in his Word, the Bible. Everything he wants to tell you is written in the pages of God's Word. If you want to hear from him, he is speaking—just open up the book and see what God wants to say to you today.

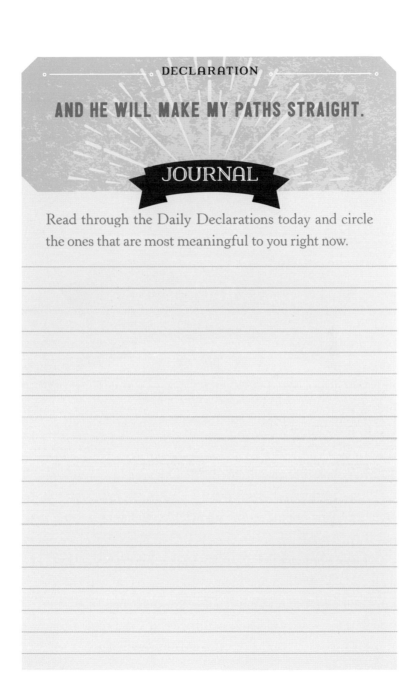

AND HE WILL MAKE MY PATHS STRAIGHT.

JOURNAL

Read through the Daily Declarations today and circle the ones that are most meaningful to you right now.

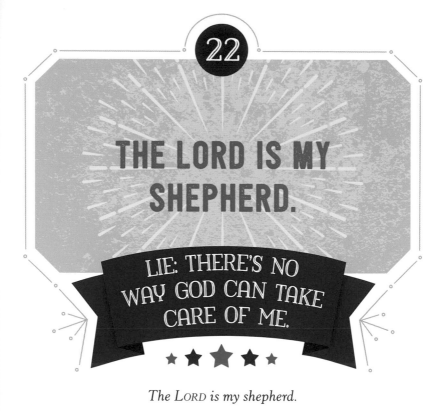

22

THE LORD IS MY SHEPHERD.

LIE: THERE'S NO WAY GOD CAN TAKE CARE OF ME.

★ ★ ★ ★ ★

The LORD is my shepherd.

PSALM 23:1

So what do you know about sheep? Does it seem weird to you that Jesus calls his followers sheep? I mean after all, aren't sheep the least smart animal on the planet? A lot of people think that, but it's just not true. Sheep can pick their shepherd's face out of a group of photographs. How they pick I don't know, but they really do know which one their shepherd is. Did you know they can also be trained like dogs? Bet you want a sheep now, huh?

Sheep are not completely unintelligent like people think . . .

they are just defenseless. They don't have razor teeth or make scary noises to chase off predators. When was the last time *ba-a-a-ah* scared anyone? The only defense mechanism God gave sheep was living in their flock under the watchful eye of a good shepherd.

If a shepherd deserts the flock, and a sheep becomes distracted and wanders off, all the rest will follow. Why? Because the only way they can stay safe is to stay close together. Without a good shepherd, it's only a matter of time before they overeat, get ahold of some poisonous veggies, become someone's dinner, or wander into dangerous territory—all because of their God-given protection strategy: groupthink.

Have you ever felt like a sheep without a shepherd? That feeling might pop up when you start to get scared to sleep alone in your room, or to go to a friend's house without one of your parents. Maybe you've thought, "I don't think God will protect me." You feel like that because you don't think God is really there even when times get scary. But that's not true. He is omnipresent. That means he's always present. All that's left is for you to believe that you are never without the most powerful being in the universe.

> All that's left is for you to believe that you are never without the most powerful being in the universe.

God created you defenseless so that you will trust him as your defender. He is described in the Psalms as a rock, refuge, shield, and stronghold. He wants you to go to him for protection, provision, and guidance like a sheep to a shepherd (Psalm 23:1), just like King David himself.

In what area of your life have you been trying to protect

yourself instead of turning to God to defend you? The Good Shepherd wants to scoop you up in his arms where you are safe and secure. Will you let him?

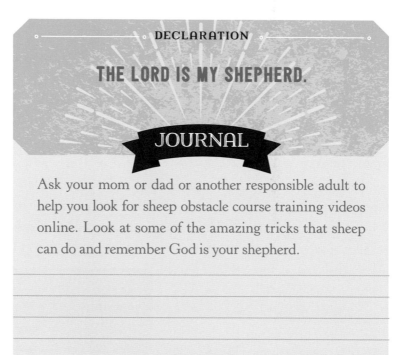

DECLARATION

THE LORD IS MY SHEPHERD.

JOURNAL

Ask your mom or dad or another responsible adult to help you look for sheep obstacle course training videos online. Look at some of the amazing tricks that sheep can do and remember God is your shepherd.

23

I DON'T NEED ANYTHING MORE THAN HE'S GIVEN ME.

LIE: THEY HAVE IT SO MUCH BETTER THAN ME.

★ ★ ★ ★ ★

I lack nothing.

PSALM 23:1

When my best friend decorated her room like the room of my dreams I was happy for her, but sad for myself. Why don't I ever get new stuff? My parents shop at Goodwill or some other secondhand stores, and my friends always get the new things. Comparing myself to others has been a pattern for me, but lately I've been learning how dangerous that is.

It's a story as old as time. We all get drawn into the comparison trap. Moses is one of the most famous people of all time. Who doesn't know about the ten commandments or the parting of the Red Sea? But as a young man he tells God he can't possibly do anything good for God because he doesn't speak very well (see Exodus 4:10).

How can Moses be so freaked out by his own inabilities and weaknesses, especially when later we hear him described as "powerful in speech and action" (see Acts 7:22). How did Moses come to believe a lie about himself?

The text tells us Moses started this agreement while he was a kid. I imagine Moses as an adopted orphan in Pharaoh's house surrounded by royals with fancy speech and clothes to match. Moses must think, "They have it so much better than me. I could never do that. I am slow of speech and tongue." Just like that, the legendary leader probably tumbled into the comparison trap.

Years later, under a canopy of stars, God asks Moses, "Who gave human beings their mouths? . . . Is it not I, the LORD? Now go; I will help you speak and will teach you what to say" (Exodus 4:11–12).

God reminds Moses that he's not walking this spinning rock alone. Moses has all he needs to do what he's been called to do, and so do you.

You might not get the best grades, or have a Pinterest-worthy bedroom, or a made for TV dog, but you are still enough because God is your Father. You can lean into the promise of Philippians 4:19: "God will meet all your needs according to the riches of his glory in Christ Jesus."

No matter where you are or what you are doing, you can always know that Christ is enough for you. You don't have to be better than everyone else or have more than they have. You have everything you need in him.

I DON'T NEED ANYTHING MORE THAN HE'S GIVEN ME.

JOURNAL

You don't need anything that God hasn't given you, that means that you lack nothing! Today, think about all that God promises you. If you aren't sure, then take a look at this list below and highlight, color, or dress up your favorite promises and truths about God and yourself.

"I am not afraid of the tens of thousands who have taken positions against me on all sides." (Psalm 3:6, GW)

"What will separate us from the love Christ has for us? Can trouble, distress, persecution, hunger, nakedness, danger, or violent death separate us from his love?" (Romans 8:35, GW)

"The Lord is near to those whose hearts are humble. He saves those whose spirits are crushed. The righteous person has many troubles, but the Lord rescues him from all of them. The Lord guards all of his bones. Not one of them is broken." (Psalm 34:18–20, GW)

"The Lord is fighting for you! So be still!" (Exodus 14:14, GW)

24

HE MAKES ME LIE DOWN IN GREEN PASTURES.

LIE: I CANNOT LIVE WITHOUT THEM.

He makes me lie down in green pastures.

PSALM 23:2

Do you ever worry about losing your parents? Have you ever freaked out because you couldn't find your favorite toy or access screen time? Fill in this blank: I cannot live without _____. I hope your heart isn't racing just thinking about this, but most kids struggle with the fear of losing something or someone they love. It's normal. You need that something or someone to protect you and to comfort you, and it's a wonderful thing to have them. But when you start to get worried about not having them around you can freak yourself out.

I have a friend who, when she was a ten-year-old, wouldn't

leave her mom—ever. She refused to go to school, she wouldn't go to her friend's house, she was totally freaked out thinking her mom might not be there when she got home. She imagined all kinds of bad things happening and she spiraled out of control. Doctors call this "catastrophizing" because you imagine a future catastrophe that you are sure will come to pass.

For me, catastrophizing often creeps in at night when I'm all alone. I worry about someone breaking into our house or my best friend turning on me, or something bad happening to my parents. If you think these things, I know exactly how you feel. You aren't alone.

So how do we get some peace and stop the stress? When I spent time with a shepherdess, I found out that sheep get stressed out too. They can't sleep if they hear a predator or hear any loud noises for that matter. That means without a good shepherd, sheep might never get any rest at all. The shepherd makes sure they are safe and can lay down and rest.

All the sheep need is to keep their eyes on the shepherd. To keep an ear out for his voice. As long as they can see or hear him they don't need to worry. They can lie down and rest.

That means that the quality of a sheep's life depends on the character of the shepherd. Bad shepherds, who don't protect their sheep, end up with skinny, sickly sheep. Good shepherds have fluffy happy sheep.

> The quality of a sheep's life depends on the character of the shepherd.

You, my little sheep, have a Good Shepherd. Jesus is your Good Shepherd. He is looking out for you.

So rest, sweet friend. Lie down and trust that your life is firmly in the palm of God. No need to worry about the worst thing that could happen or work to protect everything you love. Allow the Good Shepherd to protect what you love and to protect you.

DECLARATION

HE MAKES ME LIE DOWN IN GREEN PASTURES.

JOURNAL

Today, draw a green pasture with a bubbling brook, then draw yourself as a sheep with all your sheep family around you. Now take a look at Psalm 23. Pick a few phrases that bring you comfort and write them on your picture as you think about your Good Shepherd.

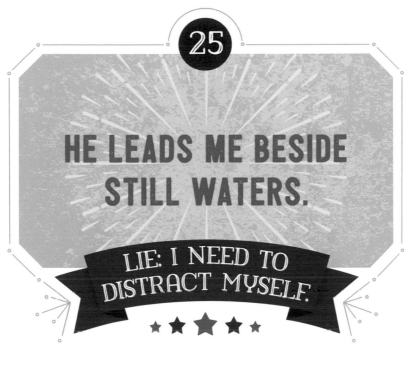

HE LEADS ME BESIDE STILL WATERS.

LIE: I NEED TO DISTRACT MYSELF.

★ ★ ★ ★ ★

He leads me beside still waters.

PSALM 23:2 (esv)

Be honest . . . are you addicted to electronics? Can you live without them? Electronics are great. They can be educational. They can be a fun way to play with friends too. But they can also be a way to distract yourself from what you are feeling, when what you are feeling needs to be dealt with.

Did you know that when you overindulge in screen time you get more easily angered, you sleep less, and you lose your concentration? Excess use of smart devices is linked to anxiety, stress, and lower emotional stability. As if that's not enough, it can actually start to destroy friendships and your time with family.

A lot of times, we reach for electronic devices to numb the pain inside. The only problem is, when you quiet the pain, you can't hear what it's saying anymore.

Every brain, without exception, needs to rest. If you deprive your brain of rest, your over-stimulated brain gets tired, unable to process pain, becomes bored, and unable to solve the problems of life. Soon all your mind can do is look for the next distraction—and quick!

> When you quiet the pain, you can't hear what it's saying anymore.

Christ wants you to step away from your distractions and to meet with him, the One who heals your soul. I know that it takes a lot of hard work to break old habits, but repetition will build new habits, habits that will help you.

Besides leading you to green pastures where you can lie down in peace, God "leads me beside still waters" (Psalm 23:2). These aren't raging waters trying to take you away from where you are. These aren't rapids that can catch you off guard and pull you in. God wants to bring you to quiet waters, the kind that give you peace and rest, that ensure you're properly hydrated and strengthened for the day and the journey ahead. His goal is to get you away from the rapid agitating waters of your screen and toward his peaceful, calm waters.

So let me ask you now, what changes do you need to make to break your electronic device addiction? Ask your parents to help you. Find other things to do with your time. Play board games, get outside and build a fort. Call a friend. Do what you can to stop the pattern of distraction and get back to the still waters of God.

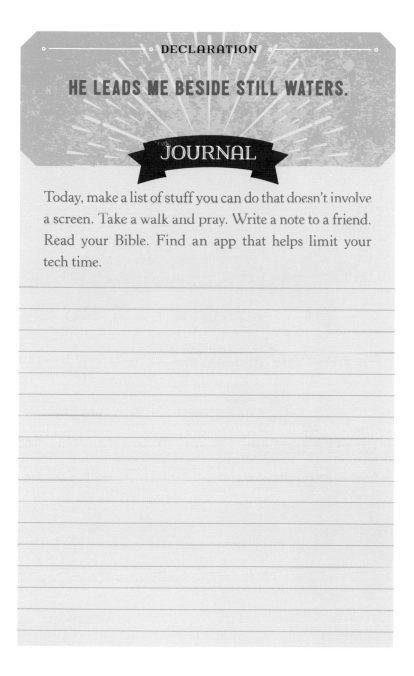

HE LEADS ME BESIDE STILL WATERS.

JOURNAL

Today, make a list of stuff you can do that doesn't involve a screen. Take a walk and pray. Write a note to a friend. Read your Bible. Find an app that helps limit your tech time.

HE RESTORES MY SOUL.

LIE: I HAVE TO BE THE BEST.

★ ★ ★ ★ ★

He restores my soul.

PSALM 23:3 (NKJV)

When I was growing up, my parents never overtly pushed me to attain particular scores on tests or win athletic trophies. Instead, they prodded me with the words, "We only expect you to do your best." So that's what I tried on everything. Trouble is, I was not the best at everything I tried. Frowny face!

Did you know that it's impossible to do your best *all* the time in *everything you do*? Nobody has the energy at all times in all situations. You need to rest, but how? How do you rest when there are so many expectations on you?

Jesus ushers us into a gentler, more joyful way of living. He invites all of us who are weary and burdened to come to him for rest (Matthew 11:28). Whenever you feel like you just can't do it if you aren't the best at it, Jesus responds with an invitation to experience his rest and restoration.

"Take my yoke upon you and learn from me, for I am gentle and humble in heart, and you will find rest for your souls. For my yoke is easy and my burden is light" (Matthew 11:29–30). A yoke is a wooden frame that's stretched across the backs of a pair of animals. It helps them to pull heavy loads or plow a field. In the ancient world, a rabbi's teaching on the Hebrew Scriptures was called a yoke. In Matthew 11, Jesus says, "Trust my interpretation of God's law and take *my* yoke upon you"—an easy yoke with a light burden. That means that if you adopt Jesus' way of living, you'll find more than a good night's sleep; you'll find rest from the constant need to be the best.

> Jesus ushers us into a gentler, more joyful way of living.

Jesus doesn't say don't obey God or your parents. He offers a relationship with him that will be the power you need to live in the fullness of truth, righteousness, holiness, and all that God intends. Best of all, you don't bear the yoke alone. He carries the heavy part for you, alongside you.

The Savior always does the heavy lifting in the life of faith. Instead of sweating to do your best in every situation, you can search for Christ in every situation and trust the work he's already doing. Take a deep breath and say yes to Jesus's invitation to rest and restore your weary soul.

HE RESTORES MY SOUL.

JOURNAL

Today, write down Psalm 23:1–3. Write it in the coolest font you know. Then spend some time memorizing it. The next time you feel overwhelmed or scared, remind yourself that God is your shepherd.

GOD IS MY STRENGTH.

LIE: GOD ONLY LOVES GOOD PEOPLE.

★ ★ ★ ★ ★

"For it is by grace you have been saved, through faith—and this is not from yourselves, it is the gift of God—not by works, so that no one can boast."

EPHESIANS 2:8–9

Are you a good kid? Do you try to do all things right so that you are loved? I know that when I do something wrong I can feel so bad. I can wonder how anyone could love me, I'm such a mess. Being good is important. It makes me, well, good. In fact, sometimes I'm not happy unless I'm better than everyone else. Being good is a good thing.

Sometimes I even feel like God won't love me if I'm not good. I mean, try to think of all the good people from the Bible. Can you think of people from the Bible stories you've heard in church who were really good and that's why God chose them? Maybe Noah. He was a righteous man. Or David. He was a man after God's own heart. They were good people, right? Obviously God loves good people. He doesn't love not good people, or does he?

I used to think I had to be something I'm not in order to be saved. In order for God, and others, to love me I had to be perfect. So I struggled to show everyone how good I was, and when I messed up I felt awful. I felt rejected by everyone who saw my mistakes. That's because I was sure that I was the power behind my goodness. I was the one who had to work at being accepted by God and by people. I was all alone in making myself a better person, an acceptable one.

This caused me a lot of stress, because you know what? I was never good enough. Then I realized the problem wasn't my inability to be perfect, it was my failure to see my being good enough isn't what saves me, God's goodness is what saves me.

> God's goodness is what saves me.

The truth is that no one is good enough, not even those good people from the Bible. They all messed up. They all did bad things, but because of God's goodness they were saved. It's called grace—God giving you more than you deserve. He didn't choose you because you were good and being good. He chose you before you even knew how to be good. Any good that you have in you is there because of who he is. So don't try too hard to prove how good you are. Prove how good *he* is. Show him to others and the love he has for you will spill over onto them.

GOD IS MY STRENGTH.

JOURNAL

Read through the Daily Declarations and write down the sayings that remind you most that God works in your weaknesses.

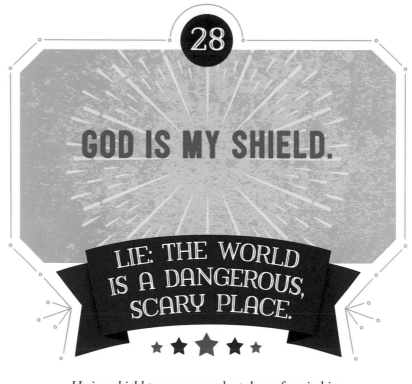

28

GOD IS MY SHIELD.

LIE: THE WORLD IS A DANGEROUS, SCARY PLACE.

He is a shield to everyone who takes refuge in him.

PROVERBS 30:5

What do you fear the most? Would you like to not fear that anymore? Living without fear is possible. God says, "Do not be afraid!" more times in the Bible than he says anything else. He says those words, or words that are close to those, 365 times. That's one for every day of the year!

In Joshua 1:5–7, God commands Joshua saying, "I will never leave you nor forsake you. *Be strong and courageous,* because you will lead these people to inherit the land I swore to their ancestors to give them. *Be strong and very courageous.*" (Joshua 1:5–7, *emphasis added*)

The Lord stood with Joshua and he stands with you. Notice your job: be strong and courageous. God repeats the instructions twice for emphasis.

But how do you have strength and courage when stuff gets scary? Joshua 1:7–8 tell us:

> Living fearless is possible for every believer in Christ.

"Be careful to obey all the law my servant Moses gave you; do not turn from it to the right or to the left, that you may be successful wherever you go. Keep this Book of the Law always on your lips."

What does obedience have to do with courage? Well, I think it's like this—when you tell God your fears and you remember his promises, you get the courage to move forward in spite of your fears. A long-dead president, Franklin Roosevelt, once said it like this, "Courage is not the absence of fear, but rather the assessment that something else is more important than fear."

When your faith in God is more important than your fear of danger, then you find courage. Remind yourself every day that God is your refuge and strength. Remember that he never sleeps or leaves your side. You are never alone—never!

When you remind yourself that God is always present and that he is always watching you, remember too that all his power is at your disposal. When you remember that every hair on our heads is numbered (Matthew 10:30), you can find comfort in knowing God pays attention to all the little things about you.

Remember, God is a shield. That means nothing happens to you without his permission and without it being for your ultimate good. Even the things you fear can be handled with confidence that God has plans for you and he loves you enough to care for you in every situation.

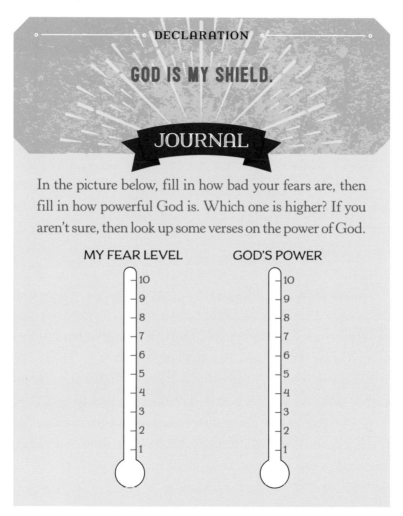

DECLARATION

GOD IS MY SHIELD.

JOURNAL

In the picture below, fill in how bad your fears are, then fill in how powerful God is. Which one is higher? If you aren't sure, then look up some verses on the power of God.

MY FEAR LEVEL

GOD'S POWER

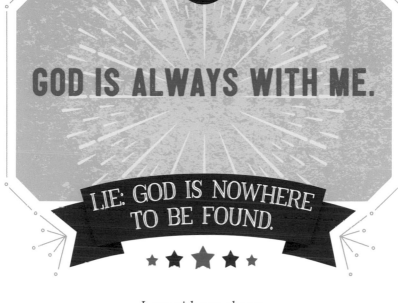

GOD IS ALWAYS WITH ME.

LIE: GOD IS NOWHERE TO BE FOUND.

★ ★ ★ ★ ★

I am with you always.

MATTHEW 28:20

When my friend Katie moved to Africa she thought it would be an exciting and wonderful journey. She was so excited to work in such an exotic location. She wanted to serve God and the people of the Congo, but she soon found out that it was going to be harder than she had ever imagined. All around her people were starving and dying from actually curable conditions like diarrhea. They didn't have clean water or indoor toilets. It was a dark place she had chosen to live. And seeing such suffering around her made her wonder where God was in all of it.

One morning, she decided to go to church. While they

were singing "How Great Is Our God," she was suddenly overwhelmed with the goodness of God. It was hard to explain, but suddenly she knew that God was there even in the midst of such poverty. The Bible promises to feed the hungry and place widows in families. But though she didn't see evidence of that around her, she knew God was there and he could be trusted. Trusted more than her own sight.

Even though it all looked so hopeless, Katie was able to say, "In the darkest of the dark, the most horrendous and heinous, God is still with us. And he calls us to be part of his great rescue plan."

You might never move to Africa, but you might find a time when you wonder where God is. In your fear, your mind might question if God really is who the Bible says he is. You might think that all those promises you've heard were just created by old dead guys to trick you. Or worse, that God is nowhere to be found. But Jesus promises to be with you always—in every moment, every situation (Matthew 28:20).

> Jesus promises to be with you always—in every moment, every situation.

In the dark in your room, in the face of a bully, God never walks out and leaves you to do it all alone. He just doesn't. Trust God's Word and trust that you aren't alone. The next time you fear, think of God saying this to you: "So do not fear, for I am with you; do not be dismayed, for I am your God. I will strengthen you and help you; I will uphold you with my righteous right hand" (Isaiah 41:10). He is with you and for you. No. Matter. What.

GOD IS ALWAYS WITH ME.

JOURNAL

Today, write down Isaiah 41:10. Write it in the coolest font you can. Then spend some time memorizing it. The next time you fear, remind yourself of this promise!

30

GOD IS ALWAYS FOR ME.

LIE: I'M ALL ALONE IN THIS WORLD.

★ ★ ★ ★ ★

This I know, that God is for me.

PSALM 56:9 (NASB)

Today, you are going to learn a saying I bet none of your friends know. "Waiting for the other shoe to drop." It's an oldie, but a goodie. In the 1800s, most apartment buildings were built with paper thin floors and walls, so thin that you could hear your upstairs neighbor drop a shoe on the floor as they got into bed. Then a second later you'd hear another shoe drop and know it was bedtime. People got used to waiting for the other shoe to drop before they knew things would quiet down for the night.

Interesting, huh? Well, today the idiom describes the feeling of waiting for something bad to happen. Have you ever done that? Have you ever thought, "Gee, life is pretty good right now. I have a feeling that means something bad is going to happen, just to even things out."

You know what happens when you are sure something bad is on its way to you? You stress out. Did you know that 85 percent of the stuff you worry about will never end up happening?[1]

You aren't alone in this negative thinking. The Israelites had seen God part the Red Sea for them to get away from the Egyptians, but they still freaked out and thought they would never survive the desert (see Exodus 16:3).

Four decades after defying the laws of nature to lead the Hebrews out of slavery, God has to remind them of his protection: "During the forty years that I led you through the wilderness, your clothes did not wear out, nor did the sandals on your feet" (Deuteronomy 29:5). God wanted the Israelites to break free from their shoe-dropping mentality—and he wants you to break free too.

> You don't have to worry about the other shoe dropping.

You don't have to worry about the other shoe dropping. You can trust in the One who travels with you and provides for you every step of the way. You can walk in the confidence that God is for you (Psalm 56:9). When you're not cowering under your bed waiting for something negative to happen, you are free to live in the hope of new miracles arising all around you.

GOD IS ALWAYS FOR ME.

JOURNAL

This week, journal about the ways God is protecting you—your parents, your house, your school, your country—stuff like that. Remind yourself in your own words how he can be trusted.

_____
_____
_____
_____
_____
_____
_____
_____
_____
_____
_____
_____
_____
_____
_____
_____
_____
_____
_____
_____
_____

31

GOD ALWAYS SEES ME.

LIE: I AM INVISIBLE.

★ ★ ★ ★ ★

For the eyes of the LORD range throughout
the earth to strengthen those whose
hearts are fully committed to him.

2 CHRONICLES 16:9

Sometimes it seems like adults can overlook your presence as a kid. Other kids can be so disinterested that you can feel like you are invisible. Have you ever tried to be heard by someone and they acted like you totally weren't there? It's the worst feeling in the world.

Few things can hurt as badly as being ignored. When you were first born you were looking for a face to recognize and to be recognized by. And as a big kid you still want to be seen and to be known. It's normal for all of us.

That sensation of being invisible can make you feel rejected and unlovable. How can people not see you and not get you? If you are naturally shy, then you know what I'm talking about. You don't have the personality to make yourself known, and so you fade into the background. You might ask yourself, *Am I here? Do I really exist? Does anyone see me?*

That's when it's easy to tell yourself, *I must be invisible. And it must be because I'm not good enough to be noticed.*

Don't believe it! The Bible says that in every situation, every moment, God sees you. There's not a bedroom, a classroom, or living room where his eyes aren't on you.

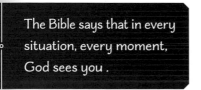

The Bible says that in every situation, every moment, God sees you .

In the story of Abram and Sarai in Genesis, there is a girl who is invisible. Her name is Hagar. She's an Egyptian servant to Sarai, who won't even speak her name. Sarai is a mean girl to Hagar. So, Hagar runs away into the wilderness, and God meets her there. Not only does the angel of God call Hagar by name, he shows how much he cares about her by asking where she's come from and where she's going. Not that he doesn't know, he just wants her to know he cares.

In this meeting, Hagar uses an expression no one else in the Bible uses. She calls God her *El Roi*, which means "the God who sees me." She is so freaked out that he sees her, notices her, cares about her, that she calls him the 'God who sees.' And that gives her the hope she needs to go on.

Like Hagar in the desert, you too can know El Roi, the God who sees you. No matter the room you find yourself in, no matter the people you are with, no matter the person you sit across from, you aren't invisible to God. He sees you.

In the space below, write all of the things that God sees in you.

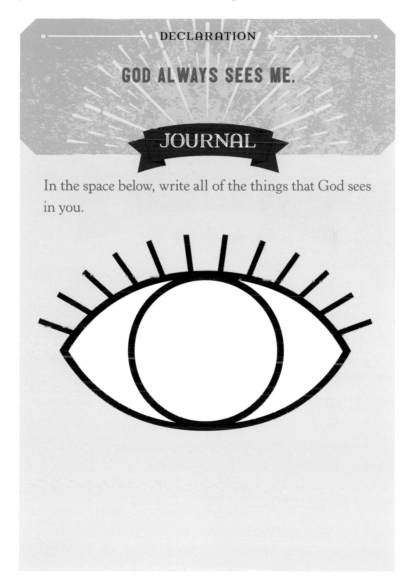

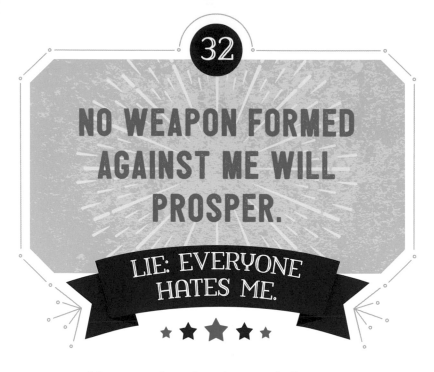

32

NO WEAPON FORMED AGAINST ME WILL PROSPER.

LIE: EVERYONE HATES ME.

★ ★ ★ ★ ★

No weapon formed against you shall prosper.

ISAIAH 54:17 (NKJV)

Have you ever failed so much, or been made fun of so much, that you asked yourself, "Why does everyone hate me?" When bad things happen to you over and over, it's easy to ask yourself, "Why me?!"

When you start to define yourself based on the bad things that happen to you, you are letting others define you. You should never be picked on by others, but we cannot always control what others do. What we can control is what we do in response. As a child, you have to tell a parent or a teacher.

After you tell someone about what's going on in your life and they have made sure there is no danger involved, we can start to talk about how to deal when the bad stuff people are doing to you isn't dangerous to your life, but dangerous to your mind. When you tell yourself that people are hurting you, even if it's your feelings and not a physical hurt, you are telling yourself that you are their victim.

The problem with that is you start to believe that life is beyond your control and that others are out to get you. This leads to all kinds of feelings of worry, fear, and even a sense that you are not safe. It steals your joy. A lot of times, when you feel victimized, you start blaming others, complaining nonstop, and throwing yourself the world's biggest pity party. But the worst thing is that when you think these victim type thoughts you give up the right to define yourself.

Are you a victim of your own making? Take this quiz to find out:

True or False

- If people don't accept me right away, they never will.
- I'll never be part of a friend group.
- I complain a lot.
- I can't change how people see me.
- I can't get over what they did to me.

If you answered true to one or more of these then you might just be making yourself into a victim. So, how do you get away from this kind of thinking? The Daily Declarations in this book combined with prayer can help set you free.

Today, remember that "No weapon forged against you will prevail, and you will refute every tongue that accuses you. This is the heritage of the servants of the Lord" (Isaiah 54:17). You are more than a victim. As God's own, you are a victor, and your name is victorious.

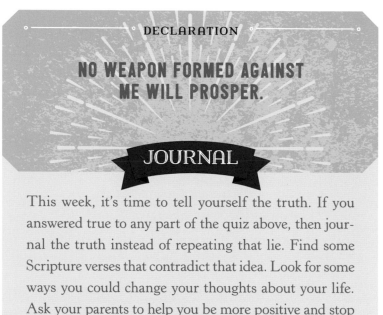

DECLARATION

NO WEAPON FORMED AGAINST ME WILL PROSPER.

JOURNAL

This week, it's time to tell yourself the truth. If you answered true to any part of the quiz above, then journal the truth instead of repeating that lie. Find some Scripture verses that contradict that idea. Look for some ways you could change your thoughts about your life. Ask your parents to help you be more positive and stop the negative self-talk.

33

I AM ANOINTED.

LIE: I CAN'T SHARE MY FAITH.

★ ★ ★ ★ ★

The Spirit of the Lord is on me, because he has
anointed me to preach good news to the poor.

LUKE 4:18 (CSB)

How many people have you told about Jesus? Or is talking about your faith kind of scary for you? It's natural to feel a little scared about sharing your faith, after all, some people think Christianity is crazy. But did you know that God has destined you to tell others about him? It's true. You have the power inside of you to talk about who God is and what Jesus has done for you and your family.

In the Bible, anointing with oil is a symbol of the power of the Holy Spirit being given to someone for a designated task. Moses anointed Aaron for the priesthood (Exodus 29:1–9). Samuel anointed kings. When Saul was anointed, the Spirit of the Lord came on him in power (1 Samuel 10:1–10). Did you know that the name for Jesus, *Messiah*, means "Anointed One?"

In Luke 4:18–19, Jesus quotes from Isaiah: "The Spirit of the Lord is on me, because he has anointed me to preach good news to the poor. He has sent me to proclaim freedom for the prisoners and recovery of sight for the blind, to set the oppressed free, to proclaim the year of the Lord's favor." That's true healing.

The same Spirit of the Lord and the same anointing to preach good news that was on Jesus, is on you. You have been anointed. You might not believe it. Maybe you haven't seen any evidence of an anointing, but it's there. All you have to do is believe in it. God has given you his power, his Holy Spirit power, to help you to do what he's called you to do—share the good news of his grace. As a child of God, you are a spiritual powerhouse of liberation and healing everywhere you go to set captives free, to restore others physically and emotionally, to usher in the wonders of God's kingdom.

> The same Spirit of the Lord and the same anointing to preach good news that was on Jesus, is on you. You have been anointed.

There might be some people who you are scared to death to share your faith with. You just know they won't listen, or worse yet, they will get mad at you. But you do not have to fear what people will do to you when you listen to God's Word. He promises to give you the power to do what he's called you to do. You are God's living testimony, anointed with the power of the Holy Spirit to bring good news everywhere you go.

I AM ANOINTED.

JOURNAL

Today, make a list of all the people you know who don't know Jesus. After you've made that list, pray and ask God to open their hearts, their ears, and their minds. Ask him to give you the chance to talk to them and share him with them.

I AM EMPOWERED.

LIE: KIDS DON'T DO THAT.

★ ★ ★ ★ ★

You will receive power when the Holy Spirit
comes on you; and you will be my witnesses in
Jerusalem, and in all Judea and Samaria, and
to the ends of the earth.

ACTS 1:8

"You're too young to do that!" Do you think that is an insult or a compliment? If you think it's an insult, then you might just have the idea that your age might get in the way of God using you. It's important to know that in the eyes of God, girls and boys are equally important and valuable. God loves and celebrates and wants to use you. You see, everyone has been given the same power of the Holy Spirit to fulfill our destiny—everyone.

Before you were born, you were given a destiny. The word destiny comes from the Latin root meaning to "make firm" or "establish." In other words, you have a God-given destination that's already prepared for you. If you think there are some things that you just can't do because of your age, then you are missing out on all God has for you.

Just think about how God showed his love, blessing, and favor on some of the kids in the Bible!

- David was still young when he took a few smooth stones and defeated Goliath.
- Mary became the mother of the Son of God! A girl, around age 13, being responsible for the King of the World!
- A young boy offered his meal to Jesus when thousands were hungry. The Lord used that kid's gift to feed multitudes.
- When the disciples tried to shoo away all the kids who were hanging around Jesus and receiving blessings, Jesus defended them and drew them closer.
- Jesus even says that those who don't receive the kingdom of God like a little child will never enter it (Luke 18:17).

Just because you're young doesn't mean that God gives you a smaller portion of his power or presence or Spirit. God gives you all he has and doesn't hold back.

> Don't give up your destiny and your access to the power of God. Your generation needs strong and determined girls and boys just like you!

Don't give up your destiny and your access to the power of God. Your generation needs strong and determined girls and boys just like you! Launch a nonprofit to save the world. Help companies make ethical, God-honoring choices. Transform your community one person at a time. Tell others about Jesus.

Gifted and empowered: that's what you are. Walk in the fullness of all God has for you.

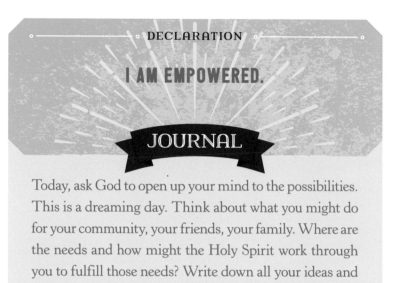

DECLARATION

I AM EMPOWERED.

JOURNAL

Today, ask God to open up your mind to the possibilities. This is a dreaming day. Think about what you might do for your community, your friends, your family. Where are the needs and how might the Holy Spirit work through you to fulfill those needs? Write down all your ideas and pray over them this week. Talk to your parents about what you'd like to do with the Lord as your strength.

35

I AM CALLED TO REACH PEOPLE WHO DON'T KNOW GOD.

LIE: I AM ASHAMED.

★ ★ ★ ★ ★

*For I am not ashamed of the gospel, because
it is the power of God that brings salvation to
everyone who believes.*

ROMANS 1.16

Is there anything that you are ashamed of? Maybe you cheated on a test or lied to your parents. Maybe you were mean to your sibling and hurt their feelings. Maybe you made a mistake and did something you now wish you hadn't done. Shame is a powerful feeling that sometimes just won't stop making you feel awful.

When you start to think things like, "I have done something bad," shame takes the giant leap and shouts, "I *am* bad!"

Whatever the source of your feelings of guilt or shame, Jesus went to the cross to get rid of it once and for all. If you feel shame over something you did that you think was a sin, you can repent and know that God immediately forgives you. No more need for shame. If you regret a bad choice you made, Jesus's forgiveness is good for that too.

No matter why you feel ashamed, Jesus went to the cross to get rid of it once and for all.

Have you accepted the grace of God, but still find yourself unable to get over the shame that you are trying to hide from everyone? How can you get the grace of God but still feel shame for what you did? Sometimes what it takes to make your heart really accept God's grace is to start telling your story and testifying about the good news of God's amazing grace to others who don't know that God will forgive them too. Maybe you have a friend or family member who doesn't understand that God's grace is always bigger than their mistakes. Maybe your best friend is feeling so bad about something she did that she cries herself to sleep. If you have experienced God's grace for your mistakes then sharing that with her might just give her the courage she needs to accept God's forgiveness for herself.

Whenever you feel that feeling of shame coming on, whether from something you did in the past or just a minute ago, it's natural to want to hide it. How embarrassing to let others see your mess ups! But keeping it quiet does not help the way you might think. It only gives your shame more power to hurt you. Instead, grab the freedom of forgiveness and let go of the shame. Share the great things God has done for you (2 Timothy 1:7–8). Proclaim it boldly. Tell your story. The world is dying to hear it.

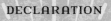

I AM CALLED TO REACH PEOPLE WHO DON'T KNOW GOD.

JOURNAL

When it comes to the mistakes you've made in the past, how forgiven do you feel today? Talk to yourself about your mistakes and God's grace as you journal today.

36

MY WORDS HAVE POWER.

LIE: WHAT I SAY DOESN'T MATTER.

★ ★ ★ ★ ★

The tongue has the power of life and death.

PROVERBS 18:21

In your friend group, are you the leader or a follower? Do you get a voice or do you do whatever your friend wants to do? It's a fine line between being bossy and being confident. Which side of the line are you on? If you have trouble speaking with confidence don't worry, that's normal for kids. It takes time to learn that what you say matters, and that there is power in your words.

James 3:2–5 says,

"For we all stumble in many ways. If someone does not stumble in what he says, he is a perfect individual, able to control the entire body as well. And if we put bits into the mouths of horses to get them to obey us, then we guide their entire bodies. Look at ships too: Though they are so large and driven by harsh winds, they are steered by a tiny rudder wherever the pilot's inclination directs. So too the tongue is a small part of the body, yet it has great pretensions. Think how small a flame sets a huge forest ablaze." (NET)

Everyone messes up. Everyone puts their foot in their mouth occasionally and says the wrong thing. You can't let the mistakes you've made in communication keep you from communicating. It's important to realize that just like learning a sport takes practice, so does speaking with confidence and with love.

Proverbs says that death and life are in the power of the tongue (Proverbs 18:21). That means that

> Just like learning a sport takes practice, so does speaking with confidence and with love.

you have a responsibility to learn to use your tongue well. It's like a weapon that can be used for good or for destruction. As a believer, it's important that you use your tongue for speaking love. So let me show you what I mean. Think words don't have the power of life or death? Read these words I've written about you:

You are a gift to the people around you. You are fun to be around. The world is better because you are in it. You help others in ways you don't even know just by being you. Your words have power. You have power; the power to build others up and to make this world a better place, just by speaking with kindness and love. Go out there and speak love.

MY WORDS HAVE POWER.

JOURNAL

Today, practice speaking love in your journal. Think of three people that you could encourage. Write down their names then list the things you could tell them about themselves that would encourage them.

I WILL LOOK FOR EVERY OPPORTUNITY TO SPEAK LIFE.

LIE: IT'S OK TO BE MEAN IF THEY STARTED IT.

★ ★ ★ ★ ★

"Do not return evil for evil or insult for insult, but instead bless others because you were called to inherit a blessing."

1 PETER 3:9 (NET)

"But he started it!"

Have you ever said that? A lot of times it's easy to think of an insult from someone else as an excuse to insult them back. It happens all the time between siblings. You know you are meant to be kind and merciful, to be gentle and peaceful, but they do something rude or inconsiderate and you just can't control yourself, you have to do it back. It's only fair, after all. You start it, I'll finish it.

But what does God have to say about this kind of justice? Is making sure everything is fair part of your job? First Peter 3:9 says, "Do not return evil for evil or insult for insult, but instead bless others because you were called to inherit a blessing." When others insult you or do mean things, getting them back is the opposite of faith. The faithful person gives something unexpected in return—they give kindness. They bless the one who's trying to curse them.

Jesus put it like this,

"But I say to you, love your enemy and pray for those who persecute you, so that you may be like your Father in heaven, since he causes the sun to rise on the evil and the good, and sends rain on the righteous and the unrighteous. For if you love those who love you, what reward do you have? Even the tax collectors do the same, don't they? And if you only greet your brothers, what more do you do? Even the Gentiles do the same, don't they? So then, be perfect, as your heavenly Father is perfect." (Matthew 5:44–48, NET)

> If you love the people who aren't being very loving to you, then you are being like Jesus.

Did you see that? It's easy to be kind to the kid who is being kind to you. Anyone can do that, even the faithless. But if you love the people who aren't being very loving to you, then you are being like Jesus. Remember God is faithful to you and loves you when you mess up, forget him, or disobey.

God knows you will never be perfect while you are here on earth, but he calls you to reach for perfection by trying to be like him. He loved you when you didn't love him, and he will continue to love you no matter what you do.

I WILL LOOK FOR EVERY OPPORTUNITY TO SPEAK LIFE.

JOURNAL

Make a list of three people who you don't like or you aren't friends with. Next to each person's name write a blessing of kind words about them.

_____

_____

_____

_____

_____

_____

_____

_____

_____

_____

_____

_____

_____

_____

_____

_____

_____

_____

_____

_____

38

I WILL SHOW COMPASSION.

LIE: THAT PERSON ANNOYS ME.

★ ★ ★ ★ ★

When Jesus landed and saw a large crowd, he had compassion on them and healed their sick.

MATTHEW 14:14

Do you know what a pet peeve is? It's something that isn't such a big deal to most people, but it drives *you* crazy. Your pet peeve might be when people come to your house and start playing with your stuff without asking. Makes you not want to invite them ever again. Or you might have a pet peeve about people who say it's time to go and then they stand around and talk for the next 30 minutes. Everyone has a pet peeve or two, and they aren't always rational.

The trouble with pet peeves is that sometimes you end up being so concerned about how you dislike something that you start to get mad at the person doing the action or think they aren't even worth your time.

In moments of frustration, it's easy to reclassify the people you're frustrated with as problems. You think the problem is with them and not with you. You don't think that maybe you have a problem with pride or selfishness. You don't think that maybe you need to learn to be patient or to think about others as more important than yourself. These are things that God wants you to learn, and in order to teach you these things he has to put you in situations where you have to practice them.

After receiving the news of John the Baptist's death, Jesus and his disciples retreat to a quiet place to rest. The crowd tracks down Jesus like a bloodhound. Exhausted and grieving, Jesus could easily consider the people annoying and bothering him when he wants to rest but, he doesn't. He looks on them with compassion and even goes so far as to heal everyone who is sick (Matthew 14:14).

The word *compassion* comes from *com* meaning "with," and *passio* meaning "suffering." To have compassion is to put yourself in another's shoes and to think from their perspective instead of your own.

Ephesians 4:29 encourages us to speak, "only what is beneficial for the building up of the one in need, that it may give grace to those who hear." That goes for thoughts in your head too. Don't let yourself cut down others, or think poorly of them. Instead have compassion on them. Think about life from their point of view, and look on them with kindness instead of harshness and correction.

I WILL SHOW COMPASSION.

JOURNAL

Write down three things that are pet peeves for you.
Why do they bother you? How can you see things from
the eyes of the person who peeves you?

39

I WILL BRING OUT THE BEST IN OTHERS.

LIE: I'M BETTER OFF BY MYSELF.

★ ★ ★ ★ ★

*"Everything you say should be kind
and well thought out so that you
know how to answer everyone."*

COLOSSIANS 4.6 (GW)

My family moved around a lot when I was a kid—from Cocoa
Beach, Florida; to Maggie Valley, North Carolina; to Steamboat
Springs, Colorado. We also lived for several years on a boat, sail-
ing from one remote island to another! Can you imagine?

I didn't have any siblings, so I was alone a lot. That gave me
time to read lots of books and make up all kinds of games. I really
wanted other kids to play with, but most of the time it was just
me, so I withdrew into myself.

After being alone for so long, I just gave up thinking I would ever have a best friend. In order to cope, I told myself the lie, *I'm better off alone.* I mean, after all, I was the only person I could count on to never let me down and to always be there.

What a lie! You are *never* better off alone. Did you hear me? *Never!*

> Yet you are *never* better off alone. Did you hear me? *Never!*

God made you for community. We can see that in the relationship of the trinity: God the Father, God the Son, and God the Holy Spirit (Genesis 1:26). God lives in community, and as humans made in his image, we are meant to as well.

In Genesis 2, God looks at Adam and says that it's not good for him to be alone. He had all the animals with him, but still God says he was alone. So he made Eve.

God makes us to have relationships with others. He makes you to have relationship with others so that you can love others and be loved. So that you can help others and be helped. So that you can serve others and be served. In healthy relationships both sides bring out the best in each other.

But even if you have a relationship where you don't benefit, it's still faithful to love and to serve those who don't know God and need to see him in you.

Now, not everyone is going to be your new BFF. Some people will only be in your life for a little while. But God has not forgotten you, and he has people for you to laugh with and play with. How can you be sure? Because community is made to help you grow in your faith: to help you grow your gifts, your talents, and your calling. And through community, you can bring out the best in others and yourself.

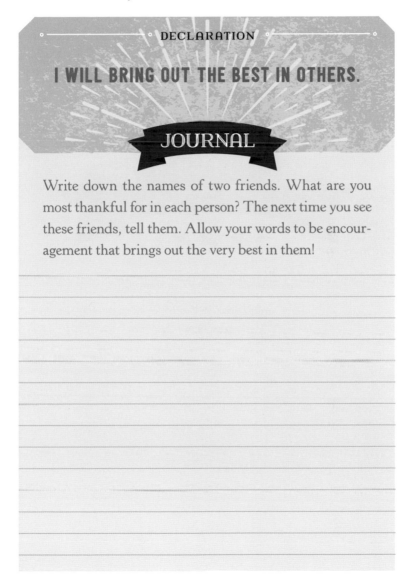

DECLARATION

I WILL BRING OUT THE BEST IN OTHERS.

JOURNAL

Write down the names of two friends. What are you most thankful for in each person? The next time you see these friends, tell them. Allow your words to be encouragement that brings out the very best in them!

40

SHAME IS NOT MY MASTER.

LIE: NO ONE CAN EVER KNOW.

*Anyone who believes in him will
never be put to shame.*

ROMANS 10:11

How do you feel about secrets? Can you keep a secret if someone swears you to secrecy? How do you feel about someone having a secret about you and not telling you? Secrets might seem like a good thing to have between friends, but secrets are not good for the body of Christ. When we keep secrets, we hide something from others. We either hide something we are ashamed of, or we hide a surprise. Of course surprises are great. They are meant to bring joy to the surprised. But when we keep a secret because we are ashamed, because we did something wrong, or we are afraid if we tell, something bad will happen, the secret is damaging. That's because the secret is something you are hiding in the dark, where no one will see, and darkness is not a safe place for your soul.

Do you know what God had at the top of his list of creation? Light (Genesis 1:3). He started to put the world together with all of its features—water, mountains, trees, animals, and man— and before he did any of that he said, "There has to be light." Now fast forward toward the end of the story, or rather the new beginning, and guess what God does? He wipes out all traces of darkness *forever* (Revelation 22:5).

All through the Bible, light signals the presence of God. In the Psalms we read about the light of God's face (Psalm 4:6), and Isaiah describes God as an "everlasting light" (Isaiah 60:19–20). When Christ gets to earth, he is the light of the world so those who believe are no longer in darkness (John 12:46).

Nature gets it. Put a plant in the dark and what happens? It dies. Plants need light to grow. And humans need it too! Light tells us when to wake up and when to go to sleep. Sometimes depressed people and people with insomnia can be made better by light therapy. Light is essential for life.

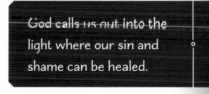

God calls us out into the light where our sin and shame can be healed.

So why is God so concerned with light? Because darkness is where we hide our secrets. It's where we go to be alone in our failure, so that no one will judge us. But God calls us to come out into the light where our sin and shame can be healed.

In order to come into the light, you must be honest about

your guilt and shame and not keep secrets where they will only grow stronger and darker. Bring it all into the light. Shame is not your master.

DECLARATION

SHAME IS NOT MY MASTER.

JOURNAL

Draw a picture of sunshine rays that represent light. Then under the rays write or draw anything that you'd like to bring out into the light before God. You can trust he already knows and he will love you as you share your heart with him.

GOD'S POWER IS PERFECTED IN MY WEAKNESS.

LIE: I NEED TO HIDE MY WEAKNESSES.

★ ★ ★ ★ ★

"[God's] power is made perfect in weakness."

2 CORINTHIANS 12:9

Who's strongest? You or your best friend? How does it make you feel to be strong? Do you like being weak? I bet I can answer that for you. No, because no one likes being weak. Weakness is not the best, it's the worst. Am I right?

It's scary to show your weakness. It's like you're a puppy and the big dogs are all running around you, and you're scared they are going to step on you, so you bark and growl and pretend like you are bigger than you really are. We are all like puppies who just want to protect themselves from the big aggressive dogs that could hurt them.

But the habit of hiding your weakness and pretending like you are strong isn't always the best. If you are afraid to be weak, then it's hard to connect with other people because they will never know the real you.

As Christians we have the perfect example of weakness as strength in Jesus. He was God but became a helpless baby. He didn't fight back when he was on trial. He didn't attack the people who put him on a cross. He was weak, and as Christians we are little Christs, that means that we can be weak. When you don't pretend like you're perfect, the power of God rests on you.

In 2 Corinthians 12:9 God says this: "My kindness is all you need. My power is strongest when you are weak." *God's power is strongest when you are weak.* If you are strong and you can do it all yourself, you don't need anyone. And if you don't need anyone, then you certainly don't need God. And if you don't need God then you must be your own savior, protector, provider, and helper.

It might seem weird to say that being weak is really being strong, but it's true. If people think your life is so great because you are smart, attractive, and strong, they will never get the picture that it isn't because of who you are but because of who he is. That means that your weakness takes the focus off you and puts it on him. That makes life not about you but about him. It makes him the God and you the servant. And others will see his power at work in you and want to know God the way you do. If you want to serve God and others, let them see your weakness and let them know that God is your strength.

GOD'S POWER IS PERFECTED IN MY WEAKNESS.

JOURNAL

In the space below, make a list of areas where you feel weak. Next to each one, write a prayer asking God to make you strong.

42

I WON'T LET UNFORGIVENESS CONTROL MY LIFE.

LIE: WHAT I DID WAS UNFORGIVABLE.

Therefore, there is now no condemnation for those who are in Christ Jesus.

ROMANS 8:1

Have you ever called yourself stupid? Have you cried yourself to sleep because you did something so bad that you just can't get over it? Guilt is a painful feeling to live with. It can make you mad, resentful, frustrated, and isolated. Guilt drives people to do some pretty stupid stuff, which is made worse by the fact that guilt is so easily gotten rid of.

Guilt is your conscience telling you you've done something wrong. It's there for a good purpose, to help you see where you messed up and to help you stop messing up. But sometimes the guilt you feel isn't really guilt but just embarrassment. When you are embarrassed, it can feel like guilt, but it's not. Guilt is what you feel when you sin against God, in other words, when you break his commandments. And God has a plan for that. It's called forgiveness.

In 1 John 1:9 it says that if you confess your sins, he is faithful and just and will forgive them. It's as easy as that. Guilt gone, forgiven, done for. But sometimes you just can't let go of it because you can't forgive yourself. Sure, God can forgive you, he's good and kind and just. But you can't forgive yourself because you know you did something wrong. Let me tell you something right now. Please pay attention to this   it will change your life. Jesus forgives you. That was the whole point of the cross. He took the punishment so you don't have to. So don't think that punishing yourself is a good idea when it's just telling Jesus that the cross wasn't enough.

Jesus forgives you

That's why Paul can write in Romans 8:1 that there is no condemnation for those who are in Christ. The condemnation, the guilt, is gone. All you have to do is confess the sin. Confess your mistake, agree with God, and then repent. Repent means to stop doing it and to do something else instead.

It is a lie to think that you cannot be forgiven. You are already forgiven. Jesus' death on the cross over 2,000 years ago achieved your forgiveness. Show yourself and the world that his sacrifice was enough by not allowing yourself to condemn yourself for what he died for.

I WON'T LET UNFORGIVENESS CONTROL MY LIFE.

JOURNAL

List the things that make you feel guilty. Then scratch them out completely as you remember that there is no condemnation for those who are in Christ. Write Romans 8:1 in your journal and think about it all this week.

43

I WILL FORGIVE OVER AND OVER AGAIN BECAUSE I AM FORGIVEN.

LIE: I JUST CAN'T FORGIVE THEM.

Jesus said to him, "I do not say to you seven times, but seventy-seven times."

MATTHEW 18:22 (ESV)

I have to confess that when someone is mean to me, hurts me, or takes what I love from me, I have a really hard time forgiving them. It just seems unfair to forgive someone who hurt me. In fact, what I'd rather do is tell anyone who will listen how mad I am at the bad person who did something I didn't like.

Of course, I'm not talking about someone who was really hurting me, like hitting me or bullying me, but about those people who hurt my feelings and make my life stressed out. I mean, I know I need to forgive those people (like my BFF who told one of my secrets to her mom and got me in trouble), but sometimes I just think when someone does something so unforgivable, I don't have to forgive them. It's justice!

But do you know what a result of my being unable to forgive was? I became distrustful. If you promised to meet me at the movie theater at 7:00 and you weren't there at 7:00, I was sure you were not coming on purpose. I got mad at everyone's little mistakes and unkindnesses and went on high alert for any meanies in my vicinity.

Then I stumbled on what felt at the time like the Bible's most annoying story. Peter wants to know how many times he needs to forgive someone. He guesses up to seven times (Matthew 18:21). That seems pretty generous to me.

But then Jesus says that's only a teeny-tiny part of how often you should forgive. He tells us to think big. We have to forgive seventy times seven! What?! Ugh!

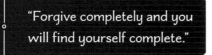
"Forgive completely and you will find yourself complete."

What Jesus says, "Forgive completely and you will find yourself complete."

Maybe that's why Jesus tells Peter to forgive seventy times seven: He knows how long it takes for us humans to offer *complete* forgiveness. For me, it seems like I don't totally forgive until like the 372nd or 379th time. When I finally stopped counting, forgiveness flooded the deep recesses of my heart. And guess what? It feels good. I'm no longer eaten up by negativity and a lust for justice. What they did was wrong, and forgiving them doesn't make it right, but my soul is healthy regardless of them.

I don't know what "they" have done to you that seems

unforgivable, but trust me, harboring a grudge is hurting you much more than it is hurting them.

I WILL FORGIVE OVER AND OVER AGAIN BECAUSE I AM FORGIVEN.

JOURNAL

Do you need to forgive someone for something they did that hurt your feelings? If you just can't get over a slight someone did to you, then let's work on that today. Write down all the people you can't seem to forgive. Then pray for them. Pray for their faith, their hope, their love, and beg God to teach you to love them the way he loves you and to forgive them.

44

I AM AN OVERCOMER.

LIE: I MIGHT AS WELL GIVE UP.

★ ★ ★ ★ ★

*For everyone born of God overcomes the world. This is
the victory that has overcome the world, even our faith.*

1 JOHN 5:4

How well do you handle being uncomfortable? Do you need
to have your own pillow or stuffy in order to sleep? Comfort
is something a lot of us have to have but don't ever really think
about. It's oftentimes what makes us say, "I can't do it. It's too
hard." Comfort is definitely something that can throw you off
your game if you don't have it.

The Apostle Paul is an expert at giving it his all in the midst
of discomfort. He knows what it's like to be in a cramped, dingy
prison cell and to still write what he needs to write.

Ancient prisons were awful places. If you were in jail back then you'd only get food if your friends or family brought it in for you, otherwise you'd starve and the people who held you there didn't give a rip.

By the time Paul writes his letter to the Philippians, it seems like everyone but Timothy has deserted him. He has every reason to believe the lie, "I might as well give up." But he doesn't.

His old friend, Epaphroditus, shows up (Philippians 2:25) and Paul is amazed. The church at Philippi didn't know about his imprisonment, but when they found out, they sent Epaphroditus to him.

This visit helps Paul to know that he is neither alone nor forgotten. With his soul refreshed, Paul writes a thank you letter to the church at Philippi:

I want you to know, brethren, that the things which happened to me have actually turned out for the furtherance of the gospel, so that it has become evident to the whole palace guard, and to all the rest, that my chains are in Christ. (Philippians 1:12–13 NKJV)

Paul didn't focus on the disgusting rats, the scary prison guards, or cramped and filthy cell. He doesn't fill them in on all the horrors of his new home. He zeroes in on the work of Christ. Like a football coach who interprets the dropped pass in a positive way at halftime, Paul argues that what looks like a major loss is leading up to a triumphant victory.

Paul doesn't let his sad feelings overcome him, and you don't

> The things which happened to me have actually turned out for the furtherance of the gospel.

have to either. Remember that comfort isn't a requirement and that you have what you need to overcome your discomfort today.

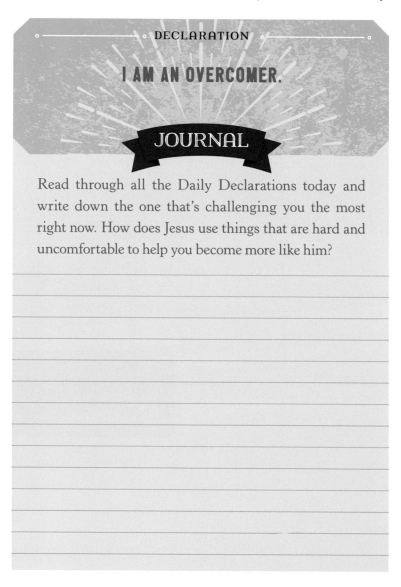

DECLARATION

I AM AN OVERCOMER.

JOURNAL

Read through all the Daily Declarations today and write down the one that's challenging you the most right now. How does Jesus use things that are hard and uncomfortable to help you become more like him?

I AM AN AMBASSADOR.

LIE: I CAN SAY WHATEVER I'M THINKING.

★ ★ ★ ★ ★

"Everything you say should be kind and well thought out so that you know how to answer everyone."

COLOSSIANS 4:6 (GW)

Sometimes I don't have a filter. I just say whatever I am thinking, and it doesn't always turn out well. Have you ever said something and as soon as you said it, wished you could take it all back? You can see your words out there making a mess of everything and you don't want anything more than to hit rewind and start over. But words are like red dye, they stain, they don't come out, no matter how hard you try. Of course, over time the color will fade, but it will take time.

Honesty is the best policy, but when your honesty isn't

carefully considered before you speak it, it just ends up being a way to be cruel without caring. Keeping it real and saying whatever is on your mind is an exercise in selfishness. Why? Because not everyone can handle what you have to say. And if what you have to say doesn't benefit anyone but you, because you get to speak your mind, then it's selfish. God wants us to love others as much as we love ourselves, that's why he says, "Everything you say should be kind and well thought out so that you know how to answer everyone" (Colossians 4:6, GW).

Is everything you say kind? Is everything you say well thought out? If your answer is no, or I don't know, then don't fret—God's Word is here to help. First Peter 4:11 says, "Whoever speaks, let it be with God's words" (1 Peter 4:11, NET). Speaking with God's words might sound impossible, and I guess it is, unless you have read God's words in the Bible and you know what he has to say.

The older you get the more you realize that you don't just live for yourself, you live for God, and living for God means that you are an ambassador, someone who represents God himself. That means that your words can't be careless and thoughtless, they have to be thoughtful and careful.

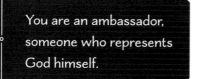

You are an ambassador, someone who represents God himself.

As a representative of God, what kinds of things could you do that would show him as the good God he is, to those around you? God's qualities, or attributes, are too many to list, but some of them are goodness, mercy, love, forgiveness, gentleness, patience, kindness. As a child of God, you are growing to be more and more like God the Father, in the way you act and the words you say. And that means that his attributes will be your attributes more and more every day.

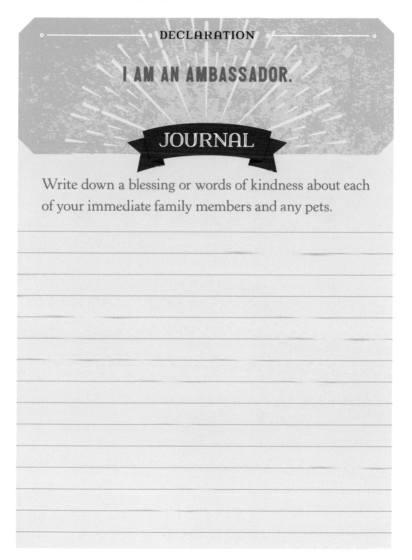

DECLARATION

I AM AN AMBASSADOR.

JOURNAL

Write down a blessing or words of kindness about each of your immediate family members and any pets.

46

I REFUSE TO LISTEN TO SATAN.

LIE: MY LIFE IS HOPELESS.

★ ★ ★ ★ ★

The thief comes only to steal and kill and destroy; I have come that they may have life, and have it to the full.

JOHN 10:10

One of my favorite games to play when I was a kid was *I Spy*. I would sit on the front porch and announce, "I spy something green." Then a series of yes or no questions followed. "Is it your shirt?" "Is it that sign?" "Is it that plant?" Until—*voilà*—the object is identified. We'd celebrate and then pick a new item for another round of *I Spy*.

Recently, that game came back to me when I was praying. I asked Jesus, "What do you spy when you see me?"

A single sentence shattered the silence: "I spy someone deeply loved."

I could feel my shoulders lower and my heartbeat slow. With those words, I was reminded that I am ever and always held in the arms of Jesus. That reminded me that Christ is with me and for us even when it seems like he's nowhere to be found.

Jesus always breathes new life, new hope, new healing into me like that. Did you know that when Christ sees you, he whispers, "I spy someone deeply loved?"

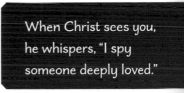
When Christ sees you, he whispers, "I spy someone deeply loved."

If you play this kind of I Spy game and you hear things like, "I spy a brat, she will always be a brat, she's never going to be lovable," you need to know you aren't hearing the voice of Jesus. You can know that because Jesus doesn't talk that way. Jesus speaks with grace and with hope. He says things like, "I came to give you life, tons and tons of life, good life, hopeful life. You are not going to stay the way you are. You are going to grow and change. You are getting better every day."

Yet you don't have to listen to the voice that says things that contradict who you are in Christ. You have the power through King Jesus, who has already won the war, to break every agreement with darkness and live as a child of light. Jesus says, "The thief comes only to steal and kill and destroy; I have come that they may have life, and have it to the full" (John 10:10). Christ comes to you with life-giving power to overcome.

You can wake up each day and say that you will not listen to the voice of Satan. That you will view the world through the lens of Christ. You can play *I Spy* with Jesus by simply asking, "God, what do you see when you look at this person?"

The answer might surprise you and set you free.

DECLARATION

I REFUSE TO LISTEN TO SATAN.

JOURNAL

Today, let's journal a game of *I Spy*. Get a pencil, get comfy, and close your eyes to pray. Ask God what he spies in you that is lovely. Let him talk to you. Then journal about this experience.

I WILL NOT FREAK OUT WHEN THINGS DON'T GO MY WAY.

LIE: BAD THINGS WILL ALWAYS HAPPEN.

★ ★ ★ ★ ★

*Dear friends, do not be surprised at the fiery
ordeal that has come on you to test you, as
though something strange were happening to you*

1 PETER 4:12

When Cinderella was little her mom died, then her dad remarried. You know the story. Then he died and left her with her evil stepmother. This story has captivated kids for decades. Her joy and kindness to everyone is amazing, considering how awful her life is. I love her as an example though, of someone who has faced so much disaster but not let it ruin her or destroy her. In fact, her joy is something that helps her make it through the darkest of nights.

You might never live a Cinderella story, but you might go through some hard times. But you don't have to freak out and get all scared . . . because you do not face it alone. Check out 2 Corinthians 4:8–9 to see what I mean: "We are hard pressed on every side, but not crushed; perplexed, but not in despair; persecuted, but not abandoned; struck down, but not destroyed."

Even when you are pressed too hard you are not crushed. If you are worried, you are not destroyed. If you are treated badly, you are not abandoned. All because you have the power of the resurrected Christ living with you. This power, which is yours through the Holy Spirit, can change you. It can help you to do far more than you ever could with only your own strength.

Through the power of Christ, your circumstances can no longer lock you up in a prison of fear and worry. Your fears of the future can no longer torture you because you know that God is still God and that he is still there. He never ever leaves you, never. Ever! You are more than an overcomer.

In that verse in 2 Corinthians, Paul isn't asking whether bad things happen to Christians. He knows they happen to everyone, but that doesn't steal his trust in God. He knows the hardships we face in life will *refine* us, but they do not have to *define* us. In every situation, we can turn to the One who saves us from being crushed and abandoned.

> The hardships we face in life may *refine* us, but they do not have to *define* us.

Your life may never ever see disaster. There is a big, very big chance nothing really bad will ever happen to you—all the more reason to stop imagining the worst and worrying about tomorrow. Why waste today on a terror that might never come, and if it does, will be made less difficult because of the love of God that is always with you?

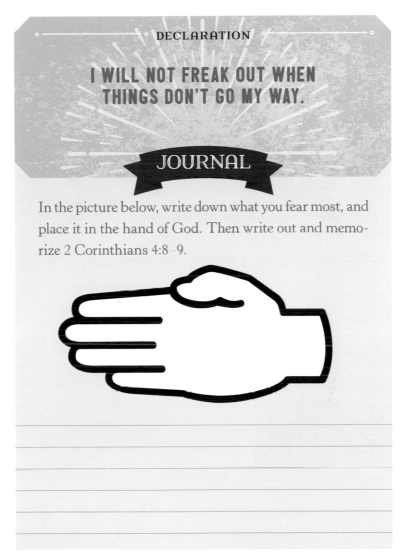

GOD WORKS ALL THINGS TOGETHER.

LIE: GOD CAN'T FIX THIS.

★ ★ ★ ★ ★

And we know that in all things God works for
the good of those who love him, who have been
called according to his purpose.

ROMANS 8:28

Have you ever felt like if one more bad thing happened you were going to scream? Sometimes things just pile up. You get up late for school. You get there and realize you forgot your homework, then you get in trouble for talking in class when all you were doing was asking about the homework.

Stuff like that seems to happen to me all of the time. It's like I'm a scoop of vanilla ice cream and trouble is the toppings at an all-you-can-eat ice cream bar. I'm drowning in trouble, and I don't know what to do. If you have ever felt like that then let me give you something that helped me out. Psalm 27:13 says: "I would have despaired unless I had believed that I would see the goodness of the LORD in the land of the living" (NASB). These are powerful words, especially if you repeat them all throughout the day. Remind yourself that you have nothing to fear and that God is good.

When life knocks you down, replace the idea that God isn't paying attention to you and what you're facing with Psalm 27:13. Instead of thinking that he's far away and has left you all alone, remember he never leaves you.

Take a deep breath and tell yourself that Jesus is still on the throne. Just because God *feels* far away doesn't mean he *is* far away. On my kitchen floor, in the middle of a good cry, I redis-covered that even when I lose my footing, God never stumbles. Not a single tear slips by his sight. Not a single groan escapes his ear.

When life catches you off guard, God remains good. He is still working all things together.

> God never stumbles. Not a single tear slips by his sight. Not a single groan escapes his ear.

That means even the hard things, the bad things, the stressful things, he is working them all together to make a good thing in you. So keep breathing and keep trusting that God will meet you wherever you need him. And you will find that what used to frustrate you and make you want to cry is leading you to God and his Word.

GOD WORKS ALL THINGS TOGETHER.

JOURNAL

Looking back at your life, what's one thing God has done in the past to show you his goodness, faithfulness, or provision. Describe in the space below.

49

GOD WORKS FOR MY GOOD.

LIE: EVERYTHING IS AGAINST ME.

★ ★ ★ ★ ★

Rise up and help us; rescue us
because of your unfailing love.

PSALM 44:26

The day began like any other. I nestled on the couch for some spiritual reflection. Our super-pup, Zoom, nestled on the back of the couch near my shoulder. All was calm and quiet and then—blurp!—Zoom stood up and threw up all over my shoulder and arm. *Ewwww!*

I went to clean myself up in the bathroom when I slipped and bonked my head on the bathroom wall. Then I realized I was late for an important phone call. In fact, I was so late I'd missed it completely.

So many things kept going wrong that day.

Exhausted after my rotten day, I cuddled up with Zoom to rest. I gazed deep into my pup's eyes with gratitude for his undying love for me. And then—blurp!—he threw up on me again. *Seriously, God? When will this stop?*

Whether it's a single bad day or a series of horrible ones that seems to have no end—Romans 8:28 reminds us that God is with us and miles ahead of us, working on our behalf.

If you're facing a hard time, today's declaration might sound cheesy or like an empty promise, but God is willing and able to redeem every situation. What you face *can* be redeemed by God for good. How can you know? Because you can see it repeatedly in the life of Christ.

> God is willing and able to redeem every situation and circumstance.

In the Gospel of Mark, it talks about the women who go to the tomb of Jesus on a dismal Sunday morning. They must have felt hopeless.

As the women arrive to care for Jesus' lifeless body, they see that the stone has been rolled away. The body, gone. Mark 16:8 describes, "Trembling and bewildered, the women went out and fled from the tomb. They said nothing to anyone, because they were afraid."

Often, it can be confusing when God doesn't behave like you expect. When you don't get the part in the play or spot on the team, it's easy to start blaming God.

In these moments, you need to remember that everything is not against you, and nothing in your life is beyond God's redemption. In God's hands, the darkness of the tomb can become a portal to new life. It's in the midst of your *Seriously, God?* moments that God can seriously work miracles.

DECLARATION

GOD WORKS FOR MY GOOD.

JOURNAL

Look up Romans 8:28 and write the verse below. What's most meaningful to you in this verse today?

GOD WORKS FOR MY GOOD AND HIS GLORY.

LIE: THERE'S NO WAY OUT.

★ ★ ★ ★ ★

"I know the plans I have for you," declares the
LORD, *"plans to prosper you and not to harm*
you, plans to give you hope and a future."

JEREMIAH 29:11

Several years ago, I traveled to spend time with a shepherd, a beekeeper, a farmer, and a vintner (someone that runs a vineyard) in order to understand the Bible's rich agricultural imagery. One of the greatest spiritual lessons I learned was from some geese wandering around a barn. They kept walking in circles. One day, I finally asked my host, "What are they looking for?"

"They're looking for their eggs," she said.

"Where are they?" I asked.

"I threw them in the creek."

My eyes bugged in disbelief. I couldn't help blurting out, "Why!?"

"Because they were not fertilized," my host said. "They would never hatch. I need to get these geese back to their regular life. They've been sitting on infertile eggs for three months. The only way to get them to the life they're supposed to be living is to take away their dead eggs."

I couldn't help but wonder how often I have sat on dreams that were never going to hatch, or worse, sat on the empty promises of the enemy that would never hatch life.

One of the greatest lies you can believe is that there's no hope, no future, unless things work out just the way you want. When it doesn't come to pass, you tell yourself that there's no way out.

But God has a hope and a future for you. In Jeremiah 29:11, the prophet reminded the people of Israel, "'For I know the plans I have for you,' declares the LORD, 'plans to prosper you and not to harm you, plans to give you hope and a future.'"

God uses his power for his people. When the Israelites find themselves pinned against the Red Sea, God splits the water and allows them to cross on dry ground. When the Philistines hem in the Israelites, God slays a giant through a stone-slinging shepherd boy. Best of all, when all of humanity is enslaved by sin and shame, God sends Jesus to save us and make us like him.

> Often, when it appears there's no way out, God displays his power.

Like those geese, you may be sitting on unhatched dreams and disappointments. But that couldn't be further from the truth.

It's time to get up and get moving. Even in this, God is working all things together for your good and his glory—that you may become more like his Son.

God invites you to release your concerns to him so you can get back to the life you were created for.

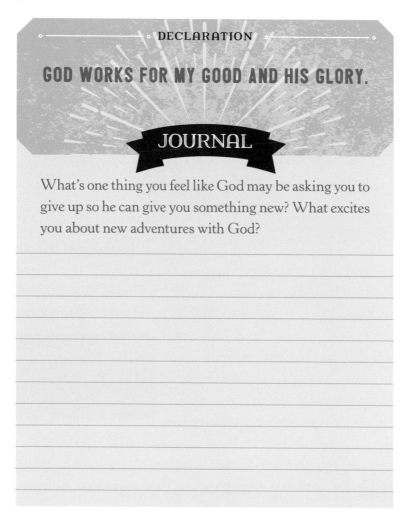

DECLARATION

GOD WORKS FOR MY GOOD AND HIS GLORY.

JOURNAL

What's one thing you feel like God may be asking you to give up so he can give you something new? What excites you about new adventures with God?

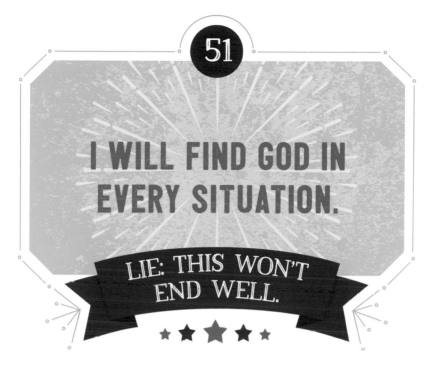

51

I WILL FIND GOD IN EVERY SITUATION.

LIE: THIS WON'T END WELL.

★ ★ ★ ★ ★

*Now to him who is able to do immeasurably
more than all we ask or imagine.*

EPHESIANS 3:20

What do you do when you get into something and realize there is no way out? Climbing the ladder to a too-high waterslide. Looking for your lost pet. Finding out your parents are splitting up. It's tempting to believe that a terrible ending to your story is not only possible but definite.

"This won't end well," you tell yourself. These words seem to have all the proof they need. So you live with them. You make room in your closet, and let fear sleep in the top bunk in your bedroom.

If you read Paul's letters in the New Testament, you will

notice that he isn't all sunshine and rainbows. This is exactly why his declarations, when he's in jail with an uncertain future, are so powerful. Paul proclaims that what has happened will turn out for his deliverance (Philippians 1:19).

Paul is riffing on the ancient book of Job. That's what Job says after he loses everything.

Job's friends surround him for seven days in silence. But on the eighth day, they open their mouths and their words sound like the Accuser. They tell Job that his wounds are his fault from hidden sin in his life.

But Job clings to the promise of rescue: "Indeed, this will turn out for my deliverance" (Job 13:16).

Centuries later, Paul proclaims the same promise leaning on two steady pillars: God's character and God's competence.

The Bible teaches that God never changes (Malachi 3:6). His purposes are unfailing, he possesses unlimited grace, goodness, power, and strength. No matter what you need, God will never run out (Philippians 4:19). Nothing is too difficult for him (Luke 1:37).

But I often second-guess his competency too. I insert myself into situations where I don't belong. I open my mouth when I should bite my tongue.

> Trusting in God's character and competence gives us the courage to proclaim with boldness, "This will turn out for my deliverance."

Each day, I must commit, "I will look for the character and competence of God in every situation."[1] This declaration forces me to search for God in life's finest details.

Even in dicey situations, Job and Paul hold fast to God as their shield, salvation, and stronghold (Psalm 18:2). Trusting in

God's character and competence gives them and us the courage to proclaim with boldness, "This will turn out for my deliverance." Declare this truth in your life and watch God transform your pessimism into positivity.

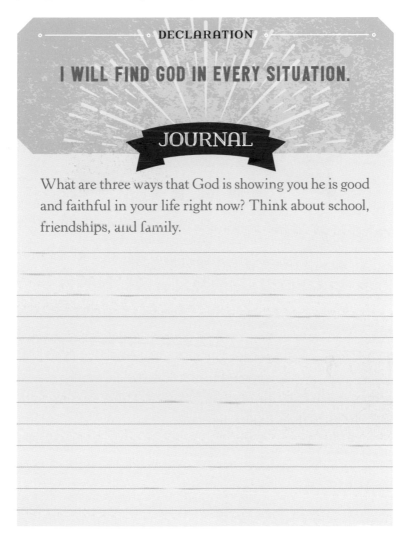

DECLARATION

I WILL FIND GOD IN EVERY SITUATION.

JOURNAL

What are three ways that God is showing you he is good and faithful in your life right now? Think about school, friendships, and family.

_____

_____

_____

_____

_____

_____

_____

_____

_____

_____

_____

_____

52

I AM ON GOD'S TEAM TODAY.

LIE: WHAT I DO DOESN'T MATTER.

★ ★ ★ ★ ★

He saw heaven being torn open and the Spirit
descending on him like a dove.

MARK 1:10

When the curtain peels back on Mark's gospel, we're greeted with a strange fellow named John the Baptizer in a camel-fur coat. We are told he has come to proclaim the impending arrival of the Chosen One, the Messiah. Without skipping a beat, Jesus himself enters the act and John baptizes him.

Just as Jesus was coming up out of the water, he saw heaven being torn open and the Spirit descending on him like a dove (Mark 1:10–11).

The Greek word Mark uses here, *schizó*, means to tear open.

This same word is used again in Mark's gospel at Christ's death. Mark describes the veil between heaven and earth being ripped open. This symbol would remind the Jewish audience of the curtain inside the temple that kept man from God.

Matthew and Luke talk about it too, but they tame their language when they retell Jesus' baptism. Instead of using the word meaning "to tear open," they use a more passive approach, using "was opened" (Matthew 3:16; Luke 3:21).

Mark uses the violent, jolting word to emphasize an important truth: at Christ's baptism and at Christ's death, heaven comes to earth. Through Christ, God tears through all that stands between us and him. God doesn't passively wait for an invitation into earth, standing on the doorstep to be let in. God is ripping open the heavens and tearing down the walls to unleash his kingdom and power on earth. The best part? It's still happening.

> Through Christ, God tears through all that stands between us and him.

The kingdom of God advances among dinner tables and church pews, in doctor's offices and cubicles, in the carpool pick-up line, and *maaaaaaybe* even while you're on hold with the customer service agent. The kingdom of God tears in whenever you allow Christ's love to saturate you and spill out onto those around you.

If you have come to believe the lie that what you do does not matter, break that assumption immediately! Do not believe for one hot minute that what you do has no impact on others. The enemy doesn't want you to play on the offensive team of God's kingdom. He wants to sideline you. Keep you on the bench.

I am on God's team today. ○ 155

But you are a kingdom bearer. You are anointed to declare good news to the poor, bind up the brokenhearted, proclaim freedom to the captives, and release prisoners from the darkness. You are on God's offensive team today, and—spoiler alert—we win!

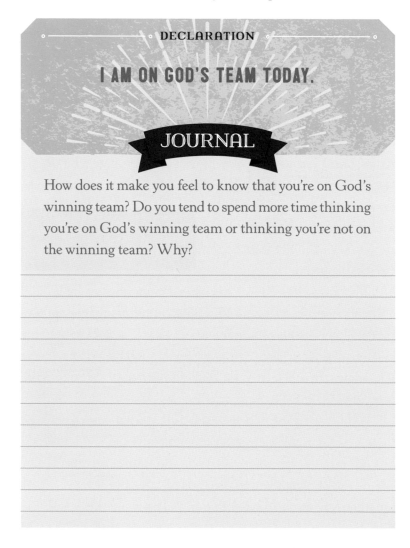

DECLARATION

I AM ON GOD'S TEAM TODAY.

JOURNAL

How does it make you feel to know that you're on God's winning team? Do you tend to spend more time thinking you're on God's winning team or thinking you're not on the winning team? Why?

THE TWO-MINUTE DAILY CHALLENGE

POWERFUL DAILY DECLARATIONS WITH SCRIPTURE

★ **Jesus is King of my life** (Exodus 20:3; Psalm 29:10–11; Acts 2:33–36; Revelation 5:11–14).

★ **I am who Christ says I am** (1 Peter 2:9; Ephesians 1:13–14; Colossians 3:3, 12).

★ **I take every thought captive** (2 Corinthians 10:5; Romans 12:2; Philippians 4:8–9; Lamentations 3:20–24).

★ **I smash every lie that enters my mind** (2 Corinthians 10:5; Isaiah 28:15–18, 29; 2 Corinthians 6:16; Hebrews 12:1–3; 1 John 5:6–12, 20).

★ **My purpose is to love, serve, glorify, and enjoy God forever** (1 John 4:19; Acts 17:28; Romans 3:23–24; Psalm 37:4; Deuteronomy 6:4–5; Matthew 22:35–40; Mark 12:28–31; Luke 10:25–28; Joshua 22:5; Psalm 100:1–5; Isaiah 61:10; 1 Corinthians 8:6, 10:31).

★ **I am filled with the Holy Spirit** (John 14:26; 1 Corinthians 6:19; Galatians 5:25; Ephesians 1:13–14; Titus 3:4–7; 2 Corinthians 1:21–22, 3:17–18).

★ **The same power that resurrected Christ from the dead lives in me** (Romans 8:11; Ephesians 1:15–23, especially 19–20; Hebrews 13:20–21).

* **I am God's kid and he thinks I'm wonderful** (Matthew 3:17; Zephaniah 3:17; Psalm 149:4; Genesis 1:26–31; Ephesians 5:1–2; Colossians 3:12; 1 Thessalonians 1:4; James 1:17–18; John 1:12–13, 14:18; 1 John 3:1–3).

* **I am fearfully and wonderfully made** (Psalm 139:14; Genesis 1:26–27, 2:7, 22), **beautiful beyond measure** (Song of Songs 4:7; 2 Corinthians 3:18; Ecclesiastes 3:11; Zechariah 9:16–17; Isaiah 61:1–3; Deuteronomy 7:6).

* **The power of God guards my thoughts** (Philippians 4:7–8; Proverbs 2:1–5, 4:20–23; 9:10), **the Word of God guides my steps** (Psalm 119:105; 2 Timothy 3:14–17; Proverbs 30:5; 1 Thessalonians 2:13; Hebrews 4:12), **and the favor of God rests on me** (Philippians 1:2; Luke 2:14; 2 Corinthians 6:2).

* **Worry is not my boss** (Matthew 6:25; Isaiah 41:10; Psalm 27:1, 42:11, 86:5–7; Philippians 4:6–7).

* **I trust in the Lord with all my heart and lean not on my understanding. In all my ways I will acknowledge him, and He will make my paths straight** (Proverbs 3:5–6; Psalm 20:7, 28:7, 91:2; Jeremiah 39:18; Nahum 1:7; Romans 15:13).

* **The Lord is my shepherd. I don't need anything more than he's given me. He makes me lie down in green pastures. He leads me beside still waters. He restores my soul** (Psalm 23:1–3; John 10:11, 14–16; Revelation 7:9–17).

* **God is my strength** (Psalm 28:7, 73:26; Nehemiah 8:10; Isaiah 40:28–31; Philippians 4:13), **my shield** (Proverbs 30:5; Psalm 3:3; Ephesians 6:16). **He's always with me** (Matthew

28:20; Luke 15:31), **always for me** (Psalm 56:9; Romans 5:8, 8:31–34), **always sees me** (2 Chronicles 16:9; Genesis 16:13–14; Psalm 33:12–15; Luke 1:46–49; 1 Samuel 16:7).

★ **No weapon formed against me will prosper** (Isaiah 54:17; Psalm 91:1–16; Ephesians 6:10–18; Isaiah 2:4; 2 Timothy 4:18; 1 Corinthians 15:50–58; 2 Corinthians 1:21; Romans 8:35–39; 2 Timothy 4:18).

★ **I am anointed, empowered, and called to reach people who don't know God** (Luke 4:18; Romans 1:16; Matthew 28:18–20; John 14:12–17; Acts 1:8; Ephesians 4:7–13; 2 Peter 1:3).

★ **My words have power** (Proverbs 18:21; Acts 15:30–34; James 5:13–16; 1 Thessalonians 5:9–11; Hebrews 3:13).

★ **I will look for every opportunity to speak life** (Proverbs 15:4; 1 Thessalonians 5:16–18), **show compassion** (Matthew 14:14; Philippians 2:1–2; Colossians 3:12), **and bring out the best in others** (Colossians 4:6; Jeremiah 29:7; 1 Corinthians 10:24; 1 Thessalonians 5:15; Philippians 1:9–10).

★ **Shame is not my master** (Romans 10:11; Romans 1:16; Isaiah 61:7; Romans 5:5, 9:3–4, 10:11; 2 Timothy 1:12; Hebrews 4:16; 1 Peter 2:6; 1 John 3:20). **God's power is perfected in my weakness** (2 Corinthians 12:9–10, 13:4; Romans 8:26; 1 Corinthians 1:26–31).

★ **I won't let unforgiveness control my life** (Romans 8:1; Acts 10:43; Ephesians 4:32; Colossians 1:13–14). **I will forgive over and over because I am forgiven** (Matthew 18:21–22; 6:12; Mark 11:25; Colossians 3:13).

* **I am an overcomer and ambassador** (1 John 5:4; Psalm 30:1–12; Romans 8:35–39; 1 Corinthians 15:54–57; Psalm 44:1–8; 1 John 2:12–14; 2 Corinthians 5:20).

* **I refuse to listen to Satan** (Colossians 1:13, John 10:10; 1 Peter 5:8–10;), **or freak out when things don't go my way** (1 Peter 4:12; Exodus 14:13; 2 Chronicles 20:17; Psalm 20:7–8; Luke 21:17; 1 Corinthians 15:58, 16:13; Philippians 1:27; 2 Thessalonians 2:15; James 5:8).

* **God works all things together for my good and his glory** (Romans 8:28; Jeremiah 29:11; Psalm 27:13; Psalm 44:26, 79:9; Isaiah 58:8; John 1:14, 17:24; Romans 5:2; 2 Corinthians 4:6, 15; 1 Peter 5:10; Revelation 21:1–5).

* **I find God in every situation** (Ephesians 3:20; Luke 1:37; Daniel 3:17–18; 1 Timothy 6:13–16; 2 Timothy 1:8–12; Hebrews 7:25).

* **I am on God's offensive team today** (Ephesians 1:13–14, 6:7; Philippians 1:21–22, 3:13–14; Galatians 6:10; Romans 14:8; 2 Timothy 4:7).

ACKNOWLEDGMENTS

Thank you to the incredible editorial and publishing team—Megan, Barbara, Sara, Jessica, Denise, and Mary. Thank you to Jonathan Merritt for being a writing iron sharpener, pushing me to be refine and rework. I'm grateful for Tracee Hackel and Andrea Townsend for their amazing editing and feedback. Thank you to Craig Groeshel for introducing me to the power of Biblical declarations. Thank you to Chris and Christy Ferebee, Carolyn and Alex Garza. Leif Oines, the love of my life, I'm so grateful for showing me such compassion and grace. Thank you to every reader who has made this journey with me.

NOTES

CHAPTER 30

1. A. Pawlowski, "How to Worry Better," NBCNews.com, December 13, 2017, https://www.nbcnews.com/better /pop-culture/praise-worry-why-fretting-can-be-good-you -ncna757016.

CHAPTER 51

1. Dallas Willard, *The Divine Conspiracy* (HarperCollins, 1998), 350.

ABOUT THE AUTHOR

Margaret Feinberg, one of America's most beloved Bible teachers, speaks at churches and leading conferences including Thrive and Women of Joy. Her books, including *Fight Back with Joy* and *Taste and See*, along with her popular Bible studies such as *Revelation: Extravagant Hope*, have sold more than one million copies and received critical acclaim as well as national media coverage from CNN, Associated Press, *USA Today*, *Los Angeles Times*, *Washington Post*, and more. She was named one of the top fifty women who are most shaping culture and the church by *Christianity Today*. Margaret savors life with her husband, Leif, in Utah and their superpup, Zoom.

Connect with Margaret at her website:

margaretfeinberg.com

Or on social media:

Instagram: @mafeinberg

Twitter: @mafeinberg

Facebook: Margaret Feinberg

Email: hello@margaretfeinberg.com

JOURNAL

JOURNAL

JOURNAL

JOURNAL

JOURNAL

JOURNAL

JOURNAL

JOURNAL

EXPERIENCE THE JOYOUS LIFE
GOD WANTS FOR YOU

Life-changing healing can be yours. And you can make it happen in only 90 seconds a day. Each of the 52 devotions in *More Power to You* by Bible teacher Margaret Feinberg examines a popular lie in our culture and invites you to replace that lie with a biblical affirmation of truth that will bring joy to your soul.

ISBN: 978-0-3104-5556-1

TASTE
and
SEE

BY
MARGARET
FEINBERG

ISBN: 9780310354864

One of America's most beloved teachers and writers, Margaret Feinberg, goes on a remarkable journey to unearth God's perspective on food.

This groundbreaking book provides a culinary exploration of Scripture. You'll descend 400 feet below ground into the frosty white caverns of a salt mine, fish on the Sea of Galilee, bake fresh matzo at Yale University, ferry to a remote island in Croatia to harvest olives, spend time with a Texas butcher known as "the meat apostle," and wander a California farm with one of the world's premier fig farmers.

With each visit, Margaret asks, "How do you read these Scriptures, not as theologians, but in light of what you do every day?" Their answers will forever change the way you read the Bible—and approach every meal.

ZONDERVAN BOOKS